THE SPIRIT OF

These brilliant studies of the art and literature of the fifteenth and sixteenth centuries reveal the Renaissance in all its variety and magnificence.

Walter Pater offers a unique insight into the personality and genius of Michelangelo, Leonardo da Vinci, Pico della Mirandola, Sandro Botticelli, Luca della Robbia, Giorgione, Joachim du Bellay.

He analyzes the talent and temperament of these great painters, philosophers, sculptors, and poets and shows how their vitality and inspiration created one of the most productive and colorful periods in the history of art.

"The Renaissance itself, with its healthier echoes of Arnold and its vision, beyond impressionism, of humanism, remains, on its own terms, stimulating as well as beautiful."

—Louis Kronenberger
from the Introduction

Other MENTOR Books of Special Interest

John MacDonald

WALTER PATER

The Renaissance

Studies in Art and Poetry

Introduction by LOUIS KRONENBERGER

A MENTOR BOOK

PUBLISHED BY THE NEW AMERICAN LIBRARY

TO C. L. S.
FEBRUARY, 1873

INTRODUCTION TO THE MENTOR EDITION
© 1959 BY THE NEW AMERICAN LIBRARY OF
WORLD LITERATURE, INC.

FIRST PRINTING, JUNE, 1959

MENTOR BOOKS *are published by*
The New American Library of World Literature, Inc.
501 Madison Avenue, New York 22, New York

PRINTED IN THE UNITED STATES OF AMERICA

CONTENTS

Introduction to the Mentor Edition

The Renaissance is among those books—they are not perilously many—in which a certain developing mood or attitude is crystallized and from which a certain school of thought or feeling proceeds. The book's very special and charming merits remain, though its original impress has by now almost wholly vanished. As *The Renaissance* was the incentive for much that came after it, so too it was in a sense the victim. It has suffered, indeed, that double fate frequent with ancestors—of itself coming to seem a little out of style; and, again, of being blamed for the faults, and taxed with the anemic blood, of its descendants. There is perhaps even a third indictment: along with those whom Pater legitimately sired and who were no great credit to him, are those ignobler ones who were designated his descendants but, even out of wedlock, never were. Of that marriage of lush estheticism and lax morals that suggests the nineties, Pater is an unwilling—and unwitting—inspiration.

The Renaissance is one of those products of the Victorian age that rejects or retorts upon what we tend to call the Victorian spirit—something massive, pious, philistine, stuffy. Swinburne, a little earlier, had shocked the strait-laced with his swooning sensuality; Gilbert, very little later, would barrage society with his rhymed irreverence. But Pater gained attention with neither irreverence nor sensuality; a scholar, a man of letters, a don, he was hardly more in revolt against Victorianism than in league with it, but was decorously outside its churchly no less than its worldly life. His "place" is rather among those celibate figures to whom Edmund Wilson has referred —Gray, Edward Fitzgerald, Lewis Carroll, Housman— who, we might say, had a walled-city experience of life; who made their own special authentic music and ordered their perhaps inwardly disordered lives. Matthew Arnold's famous remark about Gray, that "He never spoke out," applies a little to them all. And to this withdrawn and partly submerged manner, this sensitive and often feminine strain, we owe—in the absence of commanding vigor—a certain meditative, mirrorlike, slightly fussy distinction.

The earliest of Pater's books and the most read, *The Renaissance* will also, I think, be read the longest. Created largely piecemeal of magazine articles that came out over a period of years, it happily lacks anything too schematized in intention or minutely charted in movement; it possesses, instead, an intense unity of mood. Rather than formal analysis or interpretation, it suggests a beautifully arranged and not too oppressive tour of a fine, small gallery, from one related picture or mural to another, each adding its special ingredient to a cumulative effect. In one sense Pater's Renaissance is of vast duration, extending all the way from ancient Greece to Goethe: for of course it was the Greek spirit, that Hellenism "preeminent for light," that brought late-medieval Europe its Renaissance dawn; and it was what the young Goethe took, some five hundred years later, from Winckelmann, that gave the Renaissance perhaps its last faint sunset glow. In a stricter sense, Pater's book very far from compasses Renaissance thought and culture, but let us recall how modestly accurate is Pater's own title: *Studies in the History of the Renaissance*. For he has indeed ignored great figures to discourse of minor ones; and while writing notably of Renaissance painting, has hardly touched on its major literature, or its architecture or music. We get from him neither a strict organic continuity, nor a quite rich enough diversity, either—though the individual essays as much differ, in our gallery, as does a great canvas from a wash or pastel.

These "Studies" are at once scholarly and very subjective. In one sense, they show a man bringing to his subject a speculative mind, an achieved knowledge, a desire to probe and define. They offer all the paraphernalia of the historical-minded interpreter, who places religion and philosophy and ethics inside the focus of art; who indicates what makes one Renaissance figure representative, and another unique, and still another great; who indicates also what each absorbed from the Renaissance world and in turn endowed it with. But if in all this we have Pater in relation to the Renaissance, we have also in this book, and more memorably, the Renaissance in relation to Pater. For Pater has not so much used his knowledge, his intuitions, his sensibility to compass a whole cultural movement as he has distilled of that culture such particular essences as minister to his own response to art. Take, as a larger instance, his noting how religion, with the Greeks, could "transform itself into an artistic ideal"; or, in a smaller way, his noting of Botticelli that "his morality is all sympathy."

Out of such personal feelings there came, to be sure, an esthetic formulation; out of Pater's intense response to art emerged that vaunted and disputed dictum that "art comes to you proposing frankly to give nothing but the highest quality to your moments as they pass, and simply for those moments' sake." And this dictum was afterwards elevated into a doctrine of art-for-art's-sake, and the doctrine was presently vulgarized into a foolish gospel: fallen upon evil days, Pater's view of esthetics was turned into gaudily wayward daydreams. For where Pater himself simply sought, in respect of art, to divest it of any overt moral or religious or utilitarian function, but did so with high disinterestedness, others distorted it, by flashy means, toward freakish and decorative, and indeed tarnished and decadent, ends. All the same, we might as well frankly confess that Pater had sowed a seed which, expanding in a certain soil and watered at certain seasons, could hardly not produce a much too exotic flower.

But then almost every truly seminal belief can come to flower thus, or thus afterwards run to seed: where Pater beckons toward luxuriance, Pope leads to aridity; where Pater helps license the narcotic and dreamy, Wordsworth proves Scripture for the rustic and dull. In any case, the surviving virtue of *The Renaissance* is not the theory it promulgated but the temperament it expressed. It did more specific things as well: spoke up for an almost forgotten Botticelli; caught wonderfully Leonardo's "type of beauty"; explored the spirit of Hellenism and of humanism alike. *The Renaissance* can define as sensitively as it evokes; some of its definitions have been milestones in the progress of taste, and one or two remain touchstones even today. The New Criticism, I think, would not greatly quarrel with Pater's formulation of the func-

tion of art; and one could wish critics of a different sort
to ponder Pater's remark that art is "always striving to
be independent of mere intelligence." But let us not exalt
The Renaissance on the wrong grounds. For, as Edward
Thomas said, Pater was a "solitary, remote spectator of
life," a man "interested in the strangeness of effects, not
of causes"; and we might say of Pater what he says of
Winckelmann, that "his conception of art excludes that
bolder type of it which deals confidently . . . with life,
conflict, evil." *The Renaissance* is essentially an achievement—and a triumph—of temperament. To be that it
must, by so much less, be an achievement of mere intellect, or external knowledge, or generalized culture;
above all, it must boast that great instrument of temperament, a uniquely expressive style. And Pater's style is
still often marvelously precise in the very act of being
evocative and even magical. It shows still a genius for
subtle rhythms and indeed for perfect sentences. Pater's
style is the mark of his sensibility, as the essay length,
all in all, is the right measurement of his stature. His
limitations are implicit in his virtues—he is a writer fine-
boned in wrist and ankle and not quite robust in lungs
and limb. The style, with its greater powers of art than
of architecture, has not been too healthful an influence;
already in Pater—with its addiction to words like *choice,
dainty, refined;* with its tendency toward languid movement; with an exquisiteness that can verge on the too-
utterly-utter—there is an element to deplore. When
Mallock, in his once-famous novel, *The New Republic,* bur-
lesqued Pater as Mr. Rose, he had Lady Ambrose squeal:
"He always seems to talk of everybody as if they had no
clothes on." Nothing today sounds more oddly Victorian;
today, surely, any Lady Ambrose would be having him
talk of people as if they had no bodies.

But if Pater fostered, now an element of self-con-
scious plangency, now an atmosphere of pomegranates
and flutes—if he called forth in prose, among the deriva-
tive, much what a Debussy sometimes did in music— *The
Renaissance* itself, with its healthier echoes of Arnold
and its vision, beyond impressionism, of humanism, remains, on its own terms, provocative as well as beautiful.
In that seesaw in literary fashions wherein now substance
dominates and now essence, now "significance" and now

manner, *The Renaissance* must always exert a sway when its own virtues are uppermost. In a sense, there is all the more need to exert it when they are not. Even a modest allotment of art for art's sake might today have a real value, less for the old reasons than in opposition to the current reign of art for sociology's, and psychiatry's, and anthropology's, and mere cerebration's sake. Even *dainty* and *refined* might, for a little while, seem no more distasteful in the vocabulary of art than *schizoid* or *peripheral* or *in depth*.

—Louis Kronenberger

March 30, 1959

Preface

MANY attempts have been made by writers on art and poetry to define beauty in the abstract, to express it in the most general terms, to find a universal formula for it. The value of such attempts has most often been in the suggestive and penetrating things said by the way. Such discussions help us very little to enjoy what has been well done in art or poetry, to discriminate between what is more and what is less excellent in them, or to use words like beauty, excellence, art, poetry, with more meaning than they would otherwise have. Beauty, like all other qualities presented to human experience, is relative; and the definition of it becomes unmeaning and useless in proportion to its abstractness. To define beauty, not in the most abstract, but in the most concrete terms possible, to find, not a universal formula for it, but the formula which expresses most adequately this or that special manifestation of it, is the aim of the true student of æsthetics.

"To see the object as in itself it really is," has been justly said to be the aim of all true criticism whatever; and in æsthetic criticism the first step toward seeing one's object as it really is, is to know one's own impression as it really is, to discriminate it, to realize it distinctly. The objects with which æsthetic criticism deals, music, poetry, artistic and accomplished forms of human life, are indeed receptacles of so many powers or forces; they possess, like natural elements, so many virtues or qualities. What is this song or picture, this engaging personality presented in life or in a book, to *me*? What effect does it really produce on me? Does it give me pleasure? And if so, what sort or degree of pleasure? How is my nature modified by its presence, and under its influence? The answers to these questions are the original facts with which the æsthetic critic has to do; and, as in the study of light, of morals, of number, one must realize such primary data for oneself, or not at all. And he who experiences these impressions strongly, and drives directly at the discrimination and analysis of them, need not trouble himself with the abstract question what beauty is in itself, or what its exact relation to truth or experience—metaphysical questions, as unprofitable as metaphysical questions elsewhere. He may pass them all by as being, answerable or not, of no interest to him.

The æsthetic critic, then, regards all the objects with which he has to do, all works of art, and the fairer forms of nature and human life, as powers or forces producing pleasurable sensations, each of a more or less peculiar and unique kind. This influence he feels, and wishes to explain, analyzing it, and reducing it to its elements. To him, the picture, the landscape, the engaging personality in life or in a book, *La Gioconda,* the hills of Carrara, Pico of Mirandola, are valuable for their virtues, as we say in speaking of a herb, a wine, a gem; for the property each has of affecting one with a special, unique impression of pleasure. Our education becomes complete in proportion as our susceptibility to these impressions increases in depth and variety. And the function of the æsthetic critic is to distinguish, analyze, and separate from its adjuncts, the virtue by which a picture, a landscape, a fair personality in life or in a book, produces this special impression of beauty or pleasure, to indicate what the source of that impression is, and under what conditions it is experienced. His end is reached when he has disengaged that virtue, and noted it, as a chemist notes some natural element, for himself and others; and the rule for those who would reach this end is stated with great exactness in the words of a recent critic of Sainte-Beuve: *De se borner à connaître de près les belles choses, et à s'en nourrir en exquis amateurs, en humanistes accomplis.*

What is important, then, is not that the critic should possess a correct abstract definition of beauty for the intellect, but a certain kind of temperament, the power of being deeply moved by the presence of beautiful objects. He will remember always that beauty exists in many forms. To him all periods, types, schools of taste, are in themselves equal. In all ages there have been some

excellent workmen, and some excellent work done. The
question he asks is always: In whom did the stir, the
genius, the sentiment of the period find itself? Who was
the receptacle of its refinement, its elevation, its taste?
"The ages are all equal," says William Blake, "but genius
is always above its age."

Often it will require great nicety to disengage this
virtue from the commoner elements with which it may
be found in combination. Few artists, not Goethe or
Byron even, work quite cleanly, casting off all debris,
and leaving us only what the heat of their imagination
has wholly fused and transformed. Take for instance the
writings of Wordsworth. The heat of his genius, entering
into the substance of his work, has crystallized a part,
but only a part, of it; and in that great mass of verse
there is much which might well be forgotten. But scattered up and down it, sometimes fusing and transforming
entire compositions, like the stanzas on *Resolution and
Independence,* and the ode on the *Recollections of Early
Childhood,* sometimes, as if at random, turning a fine
crystal here and there, in a matter it does not wholly search
through and transform, we trace the action of his unique,
incommunicable faculty, that strange, mystical sense of a
life in natural things, and of man's life as a part of nature,
drawing strength and color and character from local influences, from the hills and streams, and from natural
sights and sounds. Well! That is the *virtue,* the active
principle in Wordsworth's poetry; and then the function
of the critic of Wordsworth is to trace that active principle,
to disengage it, to mark the degree in which it penetrates
his verse.

The subjects of the following studies are taken from the
history of the Renaissance, and touch what I think the
chief points in that complex, many-sided movement. I have
explained in the first of them what I understand by the
word, giving it a much wider scope than was intended by
those who originally used it to denote only that revival
of classical antiquity in the fifteenth century, which was
but one of many results of a general excitement and en-
lightening of the human mind, and of which the great aim
and achievements of what, as Christian art, is often falsely
opposed to the Renaissance, were another result. This
outbreak of the human spirit may be traced far into the

Middle Ages itself, with its qualities already clearly pronounced, the care for physical beauty, the worship of the
body, the breaking down of those limits which the religious
system of the Middle Ages imposed on the heart and the
imagination. I have taken as an example of this movement,
this earlier Renaissance within the Middle Ages itself, and
as an expression of its qualities, two little compositions in
early French; not because they constitute the best possible
expression of them, but because they help the unity of my
series, inasmuch as the Renaissance ends also in France, in
French poetry, in a phase of which the writings of Joachim
du Bellay are in many ways the most perfect illustration;
the Renaissance thus putting forth in France an aftermath,
a wonderful later growth, the products of which have to
the full the subtle and delicate sweetness which belong to a
refined and comely decadence; just as its earliest phases
have the freshness which belongs to all periods of growth
in art, the charm of *ascesis,* of the austere and serious
girding of the loins in youth.

But it is in Italy, in the fifteenth century, that the interest
of the Renaissance mainly lies, in that solemn fifteenth
century which can hardly be studied too much, not merely
for its positive results in the things of the intellect and the
imagination, its concrete works of art, its special and
prominent personalities, with their profound æsthetic
charm, but for its general spirit and character, for the
ethical qualities of which it is a consummate type.

The various forms of intellectual activity which together
make up the culture of an age, move for the most part
from different starting points, and by unconnected roads.
As products of the same generation they partake indeed
of a common character, and unconsciously illustrate each
other; but of the producers themselves, each group is
solitary, gaining what advantage or disadvantage there may
be in intellectual isolation. Art and poetry, philosophy and
the religious life, and that other life of refined pleasure
and action in the open places of the world, are each of
them confined to its own circle of ideas, and those who
prosecute either of them are generally little curious of the
thoughts of others. There come, however, from time to
time, eras of more favorable conditions, in which the
thoughts of men draw nearer together than is their wont,

and the many interests of the intellectual world combine
in one complete type of general culture. The fifteenth
century in Italy is one of these happier eras; and what is
sometimes said of the Age of Pericles is true of that of
Lorenzo—it is an age productive in personalities, many-
sided, centralized, complete. Here, artists and philosophers
and those whom the action of the world has elevated and
made keen do not live in isolation, but breathe a common
air, and catch light and heat from each other's thoughts.
There is a spirit of general elevation and enlightenment in
which all alike communicate. It is the unity of this spirit
which gives unity to all the various products of the Renaissance; and it is to this intimate alliance with mind, this
participation in the best thoughts which that age produced,
that the art of Italy in the fifteenth century owes much
of its grave dignity and influence.

I have added an essay on Winckelmann, as not incongruous with the studies which precede it, because Winckelmann, coming in the eighteenth century, really belongs in
spirit to an earlier age. By his enthusiasm for the things
of the intellect and the imagination for their own sake, by
his Hellenism, his lifelong struggle to attain to the Greek
spirit, he is in sympathy with the humanists of an earlier
century. He is the last fruit of the Renaissance, and explains
in a striking way its motive and tendencies.

1873

TWO EARLY FRENCH STORIES

THE history of the Renaissance ends in France and carries us away from Italy to the beautiful cities of the country of the Loire. But it was in France also, in a very important sense, that the Renaissance had begun; and French writers, who are fond of connecting the creations of Italian genius with a French origin, who tell us how Saint Francis of Assisi took not his name only, but all those notions of chivalry and romantic love which so deeply penetrated his thoughts, from a French source, how Boccaccio borrowed the outlines of his stories from the old French fabliaux, and how Dante himself expressly connects the origin of the art of miniature painting with the city of Paris, have often dwelt on this notion of a Renaissance in the end of the twelfth, and the beginning of the thirteenth century—a Renaissance within the limits of the Middle Ages, a brilliant but in part abortive effort to do for human life and the human mind what was afterward done in the fifteenth. The word Renaissance, indeed, is now generally used to denote not merely that revival of classical antiquity which took place in the fifteenth century, and to which the word was first applied, but a whole complex movement, of which that revival of classical antiquity was but one element or symptom. For us, the Renaissance is the name of a many-sided but yet united movement, in which the love of the things of the intellect and the imagination for their own sake, the desire for a more liberal and comely way of conceiving life, make themselves felt, urging those who experience this desire to search out first one and then another means of intellectual or imaginative enjoyment, and directing them not merely to the discovery of old and forgotten sources of this enjoyment, but to divine new sources of it, new experiences, new subjects of poetry, new forms of art. Of this feeling there was a great outbreak in the end of the twelfth, and the beginning of the following century. Here and there, under rare and happy conditions, in pointed architecture, in the doctrines of romantic love, in the poetry of Provence, the rude strength of the Middle Ages turns to sweetness; and the taste for sweetness generated there becomes the seed of the classical revival in it, prompting it constantly to seek after the springs of perfect sweetness in the Hellenic world. And coming after a long period in which this instinct had been crushed, that true Dark Ages, in which so many sources of intellectual and imaginative enjoyment had actually disappeared, this outbreak is rightly called a Renaissance, a revival.

Theories which bring into connection with each other modes of thought and feeling, periods of taste, forms of art and poetry, which the narrowness of men's minds constantly tends to oppose to each other, have a great stimulus for the intellect, and are almost always worth understanding. It is so with this theory of a Renaissance within the Middle Ages, which seeks to establish a continuity between the most characteristic work of the Middle Ages, the sculpture of Chartres and the windows of Le Mans, and the work of the later Renaissance, the work of Jean Cousin and Germain Pilon, and thus heals that rupture between the Middle Ages and the Renaissance, which has so often been exaggerated. But it is not so much the ecclesiastical art of the Middle Ages, its sculpture and painting—work certainly done in a great measure for pleasure's sake, in which even a secular, a rebellious spirit often betrays itself—but rather the profane poetry of the Middle Ages, the poetry of Provence, and the magnificent aftergrowth of that poetry in Italy and France, which those French writers have in view, when they speak of this Renaissance within the Middle Ages. In that poetry, earthly passion, in its intimacy, its freedom, its variety—the liberty of the heart—makes itself felt; and the name of Abélard, the great clerk and the great lover, connects the expression of this liberty of heart with the free play of human intelligence round all subjects presented to it, with the liberty of the intellect, as that age understood it. Everyone knows the legend of Abélard, that legend hardly less passionate, certainly not less characteristic of the Middle Ages, than the legend of Tannhäuser: how the famous and comely clerk, in whom Wisdom herself, self-possessed, pleasant, and discreet, seemed to sit enthroned, came to live in the house of a canon of the church of Notre Dame, where dwelt a girl Héloïse, believed to be the old priest's orphan niece, his love for whom he had testified by giving her an

education then unrivaled, so that rumor even asserted that,
through the knowledge of languages, enabling her to penetrate into the mysteries of the older world, she had become
a sorceress, like the Celtic druidesses; and how, as Abélard
and Héloïse sat together at home there, to refine a little
further on the nature of abstract ideas, "Love made himself of the party with them." You conceive the temptations
of the scholar, who, in that dreamy tranquillity, amid the
bright and busy spectacle of "the Island," lived in a world
of something like shadows; and how for one who knew
so well how to assign its exact value to every abstract
idea, those restraints which lie on the consciences of other
men had been relaxed. It appears that he composed many
verses in the vulgar tongue; already, the young men sang
them, on the quay below the house. Those songs, says
M. de Rémusat, were probably in the taste of the trouv-
ères, of whom he was one of the first in date, or, so to
speak, the predecessor. It is the same spirit which has
molded the famous *Letters,* written in the quaint Latin of
the Middle Ages. At the foot of that early Gothic tower,
which the next generation raised to grace the precincts of
Abélard's school, on the "mountain" of Saint Genevievc,
the historian Michelet sees in thought "a terrible assembly;
not the hearers of Abélard alone, fifty bishops, twenty
cardinals, two popes, the whole body of scholastic philosophy; not only the learned Héloïse, the teaching of languages, and the Renaissance; but Arnold of Brescia—
that is to say, the revolution." And so from the rooms of
that shadowy house by the Seine side we see that spirit
going abroad, with its qualities already well-defined, its
intimacy, its languid sweetness, its rebellion, its subtle
skill in dividing the elements of human passion, its care
for physical beauty, its worship of the body, which penetrated the early literature of Italy, and finds an echo in
Dante.

That Abélard is not mentioned in the *Divine Comedy*
may appear a singular omission to the reader of Dante,
who seems to have inwoven into the texture of his work
whatever had impressed him as either effective in color,
or spiritually significant, among the recorded incidents of
actual life. Nowhere in his great poem do we find the
name, nor so much as an allusion to the story of one
who had left so deep a mark on the philosophy of which

Dante was an eager student, of whom in the Latin Quarter, and from the lips of scholar or teacher in the University of Paris, during his sojourn among them, he can hardly have failed to hear. We can only suppose that he had indeed considered the story and the man, and had abstained from passing judgment as to his place in the scheme of "eternal justice." In the famous legend of Tannhäuser, the erring knight makes his way to Rome, to seek absolution at what was then the center of Christian religion. So soon, thought and said the pope, as the staff in his hand should bud and blossom, so soon might the soul of Tannhäuser be saved, and no sooner; and it came to pass not long after, that the dry wood of a staff which the pope had carried in his hand was covered with leaves and flowers. So, in the cloister of Godstow a petrified tree was shown, of which the nuns told that the fair Rosamond, who had died among them, had declared that, the tree being then alive and green, it would be changed into stone at the hour of her salvation. When Abélard died, like Tannhäuser, he was on his way to Rome; what might have happened had he reached his journey's end is uncertain; and it is in this uncertain twilight that his relation to the general beliefs of his age has always remained. In this, as in other things, he prefigures the character of the Renaissance, that movement in which, in various ways, the human mind wins for itself a new kingdom of feeling and sensation and thought, not opposed to, but only beyond and independent of the spiritual system then actually realized. The opposition into which Abélard is thrown, which gives its color to his career, which breaks his soul to pieces, is a no less subtle opposition than that between the mere professional, official, hireling ministers of that system, with their ignorant worship of system for its own sake, and the true child of light, the humanist with reason and heart and senses quick, as theirs were almost dead, reaching out to and attaining modes of ideal living, beyond the prescribed limits of that system, though possibly contained in essential germ within it. As always happens, the adherents of the poorer and narrower culture had no sympathy with, because no understanding of, a culture richer and more ample than their own; after the discovery of wheat they would still live upon acorns (après l'invention du blé ils voulaient encore vivre du gland); and would hear of no service to the higher needs of humanity with instruments not of their forging.

But the human spirit, bold through those needs, was too strong for them. Abélard and Héloïse write their letters—letters with a wonderful outpouring of soul—in medieval Latin; and Abélard, though he composes songs in the vulgar tongue, writes also in Latin those treatises in which he tries to find a ground of reality below the abstractions of philosophy, as one bent on trying all things by their congruity with human experience, who had felt the hand of Héloïse, and looked into her eyes, and had tested the resources of humanity in her great and energetic nature. Yet it is a little later, early in the thirteenth century, that French prose romance begins; and in one of the pretty volumes of the *Bibliothèque Elzevirienne* some of the most striking fragments of it may be found, edited with much intelligence. In one of these thirteenth-century stories, *Li Amitiez de Ami et Amile*, that free play of human affection, of the claims of which Abélard's story is an assertion, makes itself felt in the incidents of a great friendship, a friendship pure and generous, pushed to a sort of passionate exaltation, and more than faithful unto death. Such comradeship, though instances of it are to be found everywhere, is still especially a classical motive, Chaucer expressing the sentiment of it so strongly in an antique tale that one knows not whether the love of both Palamon and Arcite for Emelya, or of those two for each other, is the chiefer subject of the *Knight's Tale:*

> He cast his eye upon Emelya,
> And therwithal he bleynte and cride, ah!
> As though stongen were unto the herte.

What reader does not refer part of the bitterness of that cry to the spoiling, already foreseen, of the fair friendship, which had hitherto made the prison of the two lads sweet with its daily offices—though the friendship is saved at last?

The friendship of Amis and Amile is deepened by the romantic circumstance of an entire personal resemblance between the two heroes, so that they pass for each other again and again, and thereby into many strange adventures; that curious interest of the *Doppelgänger,* which begins among the stars with the Dioscuri, being entwined in and out through all the incidents of the story, like an outward token of the inward similitude of their souls. With this, again, like a second reflection of that inward similitude, is connected the conceit of two marvelously beautiful cups, also exactly like each other—children's cups, of wood, but adorned with gold and precious stones. These two cups, which by their resemblance help to bring the friends together at critical moments, were given to them by the pope, when he baptized them at Rome, whither their parents had taken them for that purpose, out of gratitude for their birth, and cross and recross in the narrative, serving the two heroes almost like living things, and with that well-known effect of a beautiful object kept constantly before the eye in a story or poem, in keeping sensation well awake, and giving a certain air of refinement to all the scenes into which it enters; with a heightening also of that sense of fate, which hangs so much of the shaping of human life on trivial objects, like Othello's strawberry handkerchief; and witnessing to the enjoyment of beautiful handiwork by primitive people, almost dazzled by it, so that they give it an oddly significant place among the factors of a human story.

Amis and Amile then are true to their comradeship through all trials; and at last it comes to pass that at a moment of great need Amis takes the place of Amile in a tournament for life or death. After that it happened that a leprosy fell upon Amis, so that his wife would not approach him, and wrought to strangle him; and he departed from his home, and at last prayed his servants to carry him to the house of Amile; and it is in what follows that the curious strength of the piece shows itself:

His servants, willing to do as he commanded, carried him to the place where Amile was: and they began to sound their rattles before the court of Amile's house, as lepers are accustomed to do. And when Amile heard the noise he commanded one of his servants to carry meat and bread to the sick man, and the cup which was given to him at Rome filled with good wine. And when the servant had done as he was commanded, he returned and said, Sir, if I had not thy cup in my hand, I should believe that the cup which the sick man has was thy cup, for they are alike, the one to the other, in height and fashion. And Amile said, Go quickly and bring him to me. And when he stood before his comrade he demanded of him who he was, and how he had gotten that cup. I am of Briquain le Chastel, answered Amis, and the cup was given to me by the Bishop of Rome, who baptized me. And when Amile heard that, he knew that it was his comrade Amis, who had delivered him from death, and won for him the daughter of the King of France for his wife. And straightway he fell upon him, and began to weep greatly, and kissed him. And when his wife heard that, she ran out with her hair in disarray, weeping and distressed exceedingly, for she remembered that it was he who had slain the false Ardres. And thereupon they placed him in a fair bed, and said to him, Abide with us until God's will be accomplished in thee, for all that we have is at thy service. So he and the two servants abode with them.

And it came to pass one night, when Amis and Amile lay in one chamber without other companions, that God sent his angel Raphael to Amis, who said to him, Amis, art thou asleep? And he, supposing that Amile had called him, answered and said, I am not asleep, fair comrade! And the angel said to him, Thou hast answered well, for thou art the comrade of the heavenly citizens. I am Raphael, the angel of our Lord, and am come to tell thee how thou mayest be healed; for thy prayers are heard. Thou shalt bid Amile, thy comrade, that he slay his two children and wash thee in their blood, and so thy body shall be made whole. And Amis said to him, Let not this thing be, that my comrade should become a murderer for my sake. But the angel said, It is convenient that he do this. And thereupon the angel departed.

And Amile also, as if in sleep, heard those words; and he awoke and said, Who is it, my comrade, that hath spoken to thee? And Amis answered, No man; only I have prayed to our Lord, as I am accustomed. And Amile said, Not so! but someone hath spoken to thee. Then he arose and went to the door of the chamber; and finding it shut he said, Tell me, my brother, who it was said those words to thee tonight. And Amis began

to weep greatly, and told him that it was Raphael, the
angel of the Lord, who had said to him, Amis, our
Lord commands thee that thou bid Amile to slay his
two children, and wash thee in their blood, and thou
shalt be healed of thy leprosy. And Amile was greatly
disturbed at those words, and said, I would have given
to thee my man servants and my maid servants and all
my goods, and thou feignest that an angel hath spoken
to thee that I should slay my two children. And immediately Amis began to weep and said, I know that I
have spoken to thee a terrible thing, but constrained
thereto; I pray thee cast me not away from the shelter
of thy house. And Amile answered that what he had
covenanted with him, that he would perform, unto the
hour of his death. But I conjure thee, said he, by the
faith which there is between me and thee, and by our
comradeship, and by the baptism which we received together at Rome, that thou tell me whether it was man or
angel said that to thee. And Amis answered, So truly
as an angel has spoken to me this night, so may God
deliver me from my infirmity!

Then Amile began to weep in secret, and thought
within himself: If this man was ready to die before
the king for me, shall I not for him slay my children?
Shall I not keep faith with him who was faithful to
me even unto death? And Amile tarried no longer, but
departed to the chamber of his wife, and bade her go
hear the sacred office. And he took a sword, and went
to the bed where the children were lying, and found
them asleep. And he lay down over them and began to
weep bitterly and said, Hath any man yet heard of a
father who of his own will slew his children? Alas!
my children! I am no longer your father, but your cruel
murderer.

And the children awoke at the tears of their father,
which fell upon them; and they looked up into his
face and began to laugh. And as they were of the age
of about three years, he said, Your laughing will be
turned into tears, for your innocent blood must now
be shed, and therewith he cut off their heads. Then he
laid them back in the bed, and put the heads upon the
bodies, and covered them as though they were sleeping:
and with the blood which he had taken he washed his

*comrade, and said, Lord Jesus Christ, who hast com-
manded men to keep faith on earth, and didst heal the
leper by thy word, cleanse now my comrade, for whose
love I have shed the blood of my children.*

*Then Amis was cleansed of his leprosy. And Amile
clothed his companion in his best robes; and as they went
to the church to give thanks, the bells, by the will of God,
rang of their own accord. And when the people of the
city heard them, they ran together to see the marvel.
And the wife of Amile, when she saw Amis and Amile
coming, began to ask which of the twain was her husband, and said, I know well the vesture of them both,
but I know not which of them is Amile. And Amile said
to her, I am Amile, and my companion is Amis, who
is healed of his sickness. And she was full of wonder,
and desired to know in what manner he was healed.
Give thanks to our Lord, answered Amile, but trouble
not thyself as to the manner of the healing.*

*Now neither the father nor the mother had yet en-
tered where the children were; but the father sighed
heavily because of their death, and the mother asked
for them, that they might rejoice together; but Amile
said, Dame, let the children sleep. And it was already
the hour of Tierce. And going in alone to the children,
to weep over them, he found them playing in the bed;
only, in the place of the sword cuts about their throats,
was, as it were, a thread of crimson. And he took them
in his arms and carried them to his wife and said,
Rejoice greatly, for thy children whom I had slain by the
commandment of the angel are alive, and by their blood
is Amis healed.*

There, as I said, is the strength of the old French
story. For the Renaissance has not only the sweetness
which it derives from the classical world, but also
that curious strength of which there are great resources
in the true Middle Ages. And as I have illustrated the
early strength of the Renaissance by the story of Amis
and Amile, a story which comes from the north, in
which even a certain racy Teutonic flavor is perceptible,
so I shall illustrate that other element of its early sweetness, a languid excess of sweetness even, by another
story printed in the same volume of the *Bibliothèque*

Elzevirienne, and of about the same date, a story which comes, characteristically, from the south, and connects itself with the literature of Provence.

The central love poetry of Provence, the poetry of the *tenson* and the *aubade,* of Bernard de Ventadour and Pierre Vidal, is poetry for the few, for the elect and peculiar people of the kingdom of sentiment. But below this intenser poetry, there was probably a wide range of literature, less serious and elevated, reaching, by lightness of form and comparative homeliness of interest, an audience which the concentrated passion of those higher lyrics left untouched. This literature has long since perished, or lives only in later French or Italian versions. One such version, the only representative of its species, M. Fauriel thought he detected in the story of *Aucassin et Nicolette,* written in the French of the latter half of the thirteenth century, and preserved in a unique manuscript, in the national library of Paris; and there were reasons which made him divine for it a still more ancient ancestry, traces in it of an Arabian origin, as in a leaf lost out of some early Arabian Nights. The little book loses none of its interest by the criticism which finds in it only a traditional subject, handed on from one people to another; for after passing thus from hand to hand, its outline is still clear and its surface untarnished; and, like many other stories, books, literary and artistic conceptions of the Middle Ages, it has come to have in this way a sort of personal history, almost as full of risk and adventure as that of its own heroes. The writer himself calls the piece a chante-fable, a tale told in prose, but with its incidents and sentiment helped forward by songs, inserted at irregular intervals. In the junctions of the story itself there are signs of roughness and want of skill, which make one suspect that the prose was only put together to connect a series of songs—a series of songs so moving and attractive that people wished to heighten and dignify their effect by a regular framework or setting. Yet the songs themselves are of the simplest kind, not rhymed even, but only imperfectly assonant, stanzas of twenty or thirty lines apiece, all ending with a similar vowel sound. And here, as elsewhere in that early poetry, much of the interest is in the spectacle of the formation of a new artistic sense. A new music is arising, the music of rhymed poetry, and in the songs of Aucassin and Nicolette, which seem always on the point of passing into true rhyme, but which halt somehow, and can never quite take flight, you see people just growing aware of the elements of a new music in their possession, and anticipating how pleasant such music might become. The piece was probably intended to be recited by a company of trained performers, many of whom, at least for the lesser parts, were probably children. The songs are introduced by the rubric, *Or se cante—ici on chante;* and each division of prose by the rubric, *Or dient et content et fabloient—ici on conte.* The musical notes of part of the songs have been preserved; and some of the details are so descriptive that they suggested to M. Fauriel the notion that the words had been accompanied throughout by dramatic action. That mixture of simplicity and refinement, which he was surprised to find in a composition of the thirteenth century, is shown sometimes in the turn given to some passing expression or remark; thus, "the Count de Garins was old and frail, his time was over" (*Li quens Garins de Beaucaire estoit vix et frales; si avoit son tans trespassè*). And then, all is so realized! One still sees the ancient *forest of Gatine,* with its disused roads grown deep with grass, and the place where seven roads meet *(u a forkeut set cemin qui s'en vont par le païs);* we hear the lighthearted country people calling each other by their rustic names, and putting forward, as their spokesman, one among them who is more eloquent and ready than the rest—*li un qui plus fu enparlés des autres;* for the little book has its burlesque too, so that one hears the faint, faroff laughter still. Rough as it is, the piece has certainly this high quality of poetry, that it aims at a purely artistic effect. Its subject is a great sorrow, yet it claims to be a thing of joy and refreshment, to be entertained not for its matter only, but chiefly for its manner; it is *cortois,* it tells us, *et bien assis.*

For the student of manners, and of the old French language and literature, it has much interest of a purely antiquarian order. To say of an ancient literary composition that it has an antiquarian interest often means that it has no distinct aesthetic interest for the reader of today. Antiquarianism, by a purely historical effort, by putting its object in perspective, and setting the reader in a certain point of view, from which what gave pleasure to the past is pleasurable for him also, may often add greatly to the charm we receive from ancient literature. But the first condition of such aid must be a real, direct, aesthetic charm in the thing itself; unless it has that charm, unless some purely artistic quality went to its original making, no merely antiquarian effort can ever give it an aesthetic value, or make it a proper subject of aesthetic criticism. These qualities, when they exist, it is always pleasant to define, and discriminate from the sort of borrowed interest which an old play, or an old story, may very likely acquire through a true antiquarianism. The story of Aucassin and Nicolette has some of these qualities. Aucassin, the only son of Count Garins of Beaucaire, is passionately in love with Nicolette, a beautiful girl of unknown parentage, bought of the Saracens, whom his father will not permit him to marry. The story turns on the adventures of these two lovers, until at the end of the piece their mutual fidelity is rewarded. These adventures are of the simplest sort, adventures which seem to be chosen for the happy occasion they afford of keeping the eye of the fancy, perhaps the outward eye, fixed on pleasant objects, a garden, a ruined tower, the little hut of flowers which Nicolette constructs in the forest, whither she has escaped from her enemies, as a token to Aucassin that she has passed that way. All the charm of the piece is in its details, in a turn of peculiar lightness and grace given to the situations and traits of sentiment, especially in its quaint fragments of early French prose.

All through it one feels the influence of that faint air of overwrought delicacy, almost of wantonness, which was so strong a characteristic of the poetry of the troubadours. The troubadours themselves were often men of great rank; they wrote for an exclusive audience, people of much leisure and great refinement, and they came to value a type of personal beauty which has in it but little of the influence of the open air and sunshine. There is a languid Eastern deliciousness in the very scenery of the story, the full-blown roses, the chamber painted in some mysterious manner where Nicolette is imprisoned, the cool brown marble, the almost nameless colors, the odor of plucked grass and flowers. Nicolette herself well becomes this scenery, and is the best illustration of the quality I mean—the beautiful, weird, foreign girl, whom the shepherds take for a fay, who has the knowledge of simples, the healing and beautifying qualities of leaves and flowers, whose skillful touch heals Aucassin's sprained shoulder, so that he suddenly leaps from the ground; the mere sight of whose white flesh, as she passed the place where he lay, healed a pilgrim stricken with sore disease, so that he rose up, and returned to his own country. With this girl, Aucassin is so deeply in love that he forgets all knightly duties. At last, Nicolette is shut up to get her out of his way, and perhaps the prettiest passage in the whole piece is the fragment of prose, which describes her escape from this place:

Aucassin was put in prison, as you have heard, and Nicolette remained shut up in her chamber. It was summertime, in the month of May, when the days are warm and long and clear, and the nights coy and serene.

One night, Nicolette, lying on her bed, saw the moon shine clear through the little window, and heard the nightingale sing in the garden, and then came the memory of Aucassin, whom she so much loved. She thought of the Count Garins of Beaucaire, who so mortally hated her, and, to be rid of her, might at any moment cause her to be burned or drowned. She perceived that the old woman who kept her company was asleep; she rose and put on the fairest gown she had; she took the bed-clothes, and other pieces of stuff, and knotted them together like a cord, as far as they would go. Then she tied the end to a pillar of the window, and let herself slip down quite softly into the garden, and passed straight across it, to reach the town.

Her hair was fair, in small curls, her eyes smiling, and of a greenish-blue color, her face feat and clear, the little lips very red, the teeth small and white; and the daisies which she crushed in passing, holding her skirt high behind and before, looked dark against her feet; the girl was so white!

She came to the garden gate and opened it, and walked through the streets of Beaucaire, keeping on the dark side of the street, to avoid the light of the moon, which shone quietly in the sky. She walked as fast as she could, until she came to the tower where Aucassin was. The tower was set about with pillars, here and there. She pressed herself against one of the pillars, wrapped herself closely in her mantle, and putting her face to a chink of the tower, which was old and ruined, she heard Aucassin crying bitterly within, and when she had listened awhile she began to speak.

But scattered up and down through this lighter matter, always tinged with humor and often passing into burlesque, which makes up the general substance of the piece, there are morsels of a different quality, touches of some intenser sentiment, coming it would seem from the profound and energetic spirit of the Provençal poetry itself, to which the inspiration of the book has been referred. Let me gather up these morsels of deeper color, these expressions of the ideal intensity of love, the motive which really unites together the fragments of the little composition. Dante, the perfect flower of that ideal love, has recorded how the tyranny of that "Lord of terrible aspect" became actually physical, blinding his senses, and suspending his bodily forces. In this, Dante is but the central expression and type of experiences known well enough to the initiated, in that passionate age. Aucassin represents this ideal intensity of passion—

> *Aucassin, li biax, li blons,*
> *Li gentix, li amorous;*

—the slim, tall, debonair figure, *dansellon,* as the singers call him, with curled yellow hair, and eyes of *vair,* who faints with love, as Dante fainted, who rides all day through the forest in search of Nicolette, while the thorns tear his flesh, so that one might have traced him by the blood upon the grass, and who weeps at evening because he has not found her; who has the malady of his love, so that he neglects all knightly duties. Once he is induced to put himself at the head of his people, that they, seeing him before them, might have more heart to defend themselves; then a song relates how the sweet, grave figure goes forth to battle, in dainty, tight-laced amor. It is the very image of the Provençal love god, no longer a child, but grown to pensive youth, as Pierre Vidal met him, riding on a white horse, fair as the morning, his vestment embroidered with flowers. He rode on through the gates into the open plain beyond. But as he went, that strong malady of his love came upon him, so that the bridle fell from his hands; and like one who sleeps walking, he was carried on into the midst of his enemies, and heard them talking together how they might most conveniently kill him.

One of the strongest characteristics of that outbreak of the reason and the imagination, of that assertion of the liberty of the heart, in the Middle Ages, which I have termed a medieval Renaissance, was its antinomianism, its spirit of rebellion and revolt against the moral and religious ideas of the time. In their search after the pleasures of the senses and the imagination, in their care for beauty, in their worship of the body, people were impelled beyond the bounds of the Christian ideal; and their love became sometimes a strange idolatry, a strange rival religion. It was the return of that ancient Venus, not dead, but only hidden for a time in the caves of the Venusberg, of those old pagan gods still going to and fro on the earth, under all sorts of disguises. The perfection of culture is not rebellion but peace; only when it has realized a deep moral stillness has it really reached its end. But often on the way to that end there is room for a noble antinomianism. This element in the Middle Ages, so often ignored by those writers on it, who have said so much of the "Ages of Faith," this rebellious and antinomian element, the recognition of which has made the delineation of the Middle Ages by the writers of the Romantic school in France, by Victor Hugo for instance, in *Notre-Dame de Paris,* so suggestive and exciting, is found alike in the history of Abélard and the legend of Tannhäuser. More and more, as we come to mark changes, and distinctions of temper, in what is often in one all-embracing confusion called the Middle Ages, this rebellious element, this sinister claim for liberty of heart and thought, comes

to the surface. The Albigensian movement, connected
so strangely with the history of Provençal poetry, is
deeply tinged with it. A touch of it makes the Fran-
ciscan order, with its poetry, its mysticism, its *illumi-
nation,* from the point of view of religious authority,
justly suspect. It influences the thoughts of those obscure
prophetical writers, like Joachin of Flora, strange dream-
ers in a world of flowery rhetoric of that third and final
dispensation of a spirit of freedom, in which law has
passed away. Of this spirit *Aucassin et Nicolette* contains perhaps the most famous expression; it is the
answer Aucassin gives when he is threatened with the
pains of hell if he makes Nicolette his mistress. A
creature wholly of affection and the senses, he sees on
the way to paradise only a feeble company of aged
priests, "clinging day and night to the chapel altars,"
barefoot or in patched sandals. With or even without
Nicolette, "his sweet mistress whom he so much loves,"
he, for his part, is ready to start on the way to hell,
along with "the good scholars," as he says, and the
actors, and the fine horsemen dead in battle, and the
men of fashion,* and "the fair courteous ladies who
had two or three chevaliers apiece beside their own
true lords," all gay with music, in their gold and silver
and beautiful furs—"the vair and the grey."

For in the *House Beautiful* the saints too have their
place; and the student of the Renaissance has this advantage over the student of the emancipation of the
human mind in the Reformation, or the French Revolution, that, in tracing the footsteps of humanity to
higher levels, he is not beset at every turn by the in-
flexibilities and antagonisms of some well-recognized controversy, with rigidly defined opposites, exhausting the
intelligence and limiting one's sympathies. That opposition of the professional defenders of a mere system to
the more sincere and generous play of the forces of
human mind and character, which I noted as the secret
of Abélard's struggle, is indeed always powerful. But the
incompatibility of souls really "fair" is not essential;
and within the enchanted region of the Renaissance,

---

* *Parage,* peerage—which came to signify all that ambitious
youth affected most on the outside of life, in that old world of
the troubadours, with whom this term is of frequent recurrence.

one needs not be forever on one's guard; here there are no fixed parties, no exclusions; all breathes of that unity of culture in which whatsoever things are comely are reconciled, for the elevation and adornment of our spirits. And just in proportion as those who took part in the Renaissance become centrally representative of it, just so much the more is this condition realized in them. The wicked popes, and the loveless tyrants, who from time to time become its patrons, or mere speculators in its fortunes, lend themselves easily to disputations, and, from this side or that, the spirit of controversy lays just hold upon them. But the painter of the *Last Supper,* with his kindred, live in a land where controversy has no breathing place, and refuse to be classified. In the story of *Aucassin et Nicolette,* in the literature which it represents, the note of defiance, of the opposition of one system to another, is sometimes harsh; let me conclude with a morsel from *Amis and Amile,* in which the harmony of human interests is still entire. For the story of the great traditional friendship, in which, as I said, the liberty of the heart makes itself felt, seems, as we have it, to have been written by a monk, *La vie des saints martyrs Amis et Amile;* it was not till the end of the seventeenth century that they were finally excluded from the martyrology, and then out of deference to a sort of modern criticism; and their story ends with this monkish miracle of earthly comradeship, more than faithful unto death.

For, as God had united them in their lives in one accord, so they were not divided in their death, falling together side by side, with a host of other brave men, in battle for King Charles, at Mortara, so called from that great slaughter. And the bishops gave counsel to the king and queen that they should bury the dead, and build a church in that place; and their counsel pleased the king greatly; and there were built there two churches, the one by commandment of the king in honor of Saint Oseige, and the other by commandment of the queen in honour of Saint Peter.

And the king caused the two chests of stone to be brought, in which the bodies of Amis and Amile lay; and Amile was carried to the church of Saint Peter, and

Amis to the church of Saint Oseige; and the other corpses were buried, some in one place and some in the other. But lo! the next morning, the body of Amile in his coffin was found lying in the church of Saint Oseige, beside the coffin of Amis his comrade. Behold then this wondrous amity, which by death could not be dissevered!

This miracle God did, who gave to his disciples power to remove mountains. And by reason of this miracle the king and queen remained in that place for a space of thirty days, and performed the offices of the dead who were slain, and honored the said churches with great gifts; and the bishop ordained many clerks to serve in the church of Saint Oseige, and commanded them that they should guard duly, with great devotion, the bodies of the two companions, Amis and Amile.

PICO DELLA MIRANDOLA

NO account of the Renaissance can be complete without some notice of the attempt made by certain Italian scholars of the fifteenth century to reconcile Christianity with the religion of ancient Greece. To reconcile forms of sentiment which at first sight seem incompatible, to adjust the various products of the human mind to each other in one many-sided type of intellectual culture, to give the human spirit, for the heart and imagination to feed upon, as much as it could possibly receive, belonged to the generous instincts of that age. An earlier and simpler generation had seen in the gods of Greece so many malignant spirits, the defeated but still living centers of the religion of darkness, struggling, not always in vain, against the kingdom of light. Little by little, as the natural charm of pagan story reasserted itself over minds emerging out of barbarism, the religious significance which had once belonged to it was lost sight of, and it came to be regarded as the subject of a purely artistic or poetical treatment. But it was inevitable that from time to time minds should arise, deeply enough impressed by its beauty and power, to ask themselves whether the religion of Greece was indeed a rival of the religion of Christ; for the older gods had rehabilitated themselves, and men's allegiance was divided. And the fifteenth century was an impassioned age, so ardent and serious in its pursuit of art that it consecrated everything with which art had to do as a religious object. The restored Greek literature had made it familiar, at least in Plato, with a style of expression about the earlier gods, which had about it much of the warmth and unction of a Christian hymn. It was too familiar with such language to regard mythology as a mere story; and it was too serious to play with a religion.

Let me briefly remind the reader—says Heine, in the *Gods in Exile,* an essay full of that strange blending of sentiment which is characteristic of the traditions of the Middle Ages concerning the pagan religions—*how the gods of the older world, at the time of the definite triumph of Christianity, that is, in the third century, fell into painful embarrassments, which greatly resembled certain tragical situations of their earlier life. They now found themselves beset by the same troublesome necessities to which they had once before been exposed during the primitive ages, in that revolutionary epoch when the Titans broke out of the custody of Orcus, and, piling Pelion on Ossa, scaled Olympus. Unfortunate gods! They had then to take flight ignominiously, and hide themselves among us here on earth, under all sorts of disguises. Most of them betook themselves to Egypt, where for greater security they assumed the forms of animals, as is generally known. Just in the same way, they had to take flight again, and seek entertainment in remote hiding places, when those iconoclastic zealots, the black brood of monks, broke down all the temples, and pursued the gods with fire and curses. Many of these unfortunate emigrants, now entirely deprived of shelter and ambrosia, must needs take to vulgar handicrafts as a means of earning their bread. In these circumstances, many whose sacred groves had been confiscated, let themselves out for hire as woodcutters in Germany, and were forced to drink beer instead of nectar. Apollo seems to have been content to take service under graziers, and as he had once kept the cows of Admetus, so he lived now as a shepherd in lower Austria. Here, however, having become suspected on ac-*

*count of his beautiful singing, he was recognized by a
learned monk as one of the old pagan gods, and handed
over to the spiritual tribunal. On the rack he confessed
that he was the god Apollo; and before his execution he
begged that he might be suffered to play once more
upon the lyre, and to sing a song. And he played so
touchingly, and sang with such magic, and was withal
so beautiful in form and feature, that all the women
wept, and many of them were so deeply impressed that
they shortly afterward fell sick. And sometime afterward the people wished to drag him from the grave again,
that a stake might be driven through his body, in the
belief that he had been a vampire, and that the sick
women would by this means recover. But they found
the grave empty.*

The Renaissance of the fifteenth century was, in many
things, great rather by what it designed than by what
it achieved. Much which it aspired to do, and did but
imperfectly or mistakenly, was accomplished in what is
called the *éclaircissement* of the eighteenth century, or
in our own generation; and what really belongs to the
revival of the fifteenth century is but the leading instinct,
the curiosity, the initiatory idea. It is so with this very
question of the reconciliation of the religion of antiquity
with the religion of Christ. A modern scholar occupied
by this problem might observe: that all religions may
be regarded as natural products; that at least in their
origin, their growth, and decay, they have common
laws, and are not to be isolated from the other movements of the human mind in the periods in which
they respectively prevailed; that they arise spontaneously
out of the human mind, as expressions of the varying
phases of its sentiment concerning the unseen world;
that every intellectual product must be judged from
the point of view of the age and the people in which
it was produced. He might go on to observe that each
has contributed something to the development of the
religious sense and, ranging them as so many stages in
the gradual education of the human mind, justify the
existence of each. The basis of the reconciliation of
the religions of the world would thus be the inexhaustible
activity and creativeness of the human mind itself, in
which all religions alike have their root, and in which

all alike are reconciled; just as the fancies of childhood
and the thoughts of old age meet and are laid to rest,
in the experience of the individual. Far different was
the method followed by the scholars of the fifteenth
century. They lacked the very rudiments of the historic
sense, which, by an imaginative act, throws itself back
into a world unlike one's own, and estimates every
intellectual creation in its connection with the age from
which it proceeded; they had no idea of development,
of the differences of ages, of the gradual education of
the human race. In their attempts to reconcile the
religions of the world, they were thus thrown back upon
the quicksand of allegorical interpretation. The religions
of the world were to be reconciled, not as successive
stages in a gradual development of the religious sense,
but as subsisting side by side, and substantially in
agreement with each other. And here, the first necessity
was to misrepresent the language, the conceptions, the
sentiments, it was proposed to compare and reconcile.
Plato and Homer must be made to speak agreeably to
Moses. Set side by side, the mere surfaces could never
unite in any harmony of design. Therefore, one must
go below the surface, and bring up the supposed secondary, or still more remote meaning, that diviner
signification held in reserve—*in recessu divinius aliquid*
—latent in some stray touch of Homer, or figure of
speech in the books of Moses.

And yet as a curiosity of the human mind, a "mad-
house cell," if you will, into which we may peep for
a moment, and see it at work weaving strange fancies,
the allegorical interpretation of the fifteenth century has
its interest. With its strange web of imagery, its quaint
conceits, its unexpected combinations and subtle mor-
alizing, it is an element in the local color of a great
age. It illustrates also the faith of that age in all oracles,
its desire to hear all voices, its generous belief that
nothing which had ever interested the human mind could
wholly lose its vitality. It is the counterpart, though
certainly the feebler counterpart, of that practical truce
and reconciliation of the gods of Greece with the Christian religion, which is seen in the art of the time; and
it is for his share in this work, and because his own
story is a sort of analogue or visible equivalent to the

expression of this purpose in his writings, that something of a general interest still belongs to the name of
Pico della Mirandola, whose life, written by his nephew
Francis, seemed worthy, for some touch of sweetness
in it, to be translated out of the original Latin by Sir
Thomas More, that great lover of Italian culture, among
whose works, this life of Pico, *Earl of Mirandola, and
a great lord of Italy,* as he calls him, may still be read,
in its quaint, antiquated English.

Marsilio Ficino has told us how Pico came to Florence.
It was the very day—some day probably in the year
1482—on which Ficino had finished his famous translation of Plato into Latin, the work to which he had been
dedicated from childhood by Cosimo de' Medici, in
furtherance of his desire to resuscitate the knowledge
of Plato among his fellow citizens. Florence indeed, as
M. Renan has pointed out, had always had an affinity
for the mystic and dreamy philosophy of Plato, while
the colder and more practical philosophy of Aristotle
had flourished in Padua, and other cities of the north;
and the Florentines, though they knew perhaps very
little about him, had had the name of the great idealist
often on their lips. To increase this knowledge, Cosimo
had founded the Platonic academy, with periodical discussions at the villa of Careggi. The fall of Constantino-
ple in 1453, and the council in 1438 for the reconciliation
of the Greek and Latin Churches, had brought to Florence many a needy Greek scholar. And now the work
was completed, the door of the mystical temple lay
open to all who could construe Latin, and the scholar
rested from his labor; when there was introduced into
his study, where a lamp burned continually before the
bust of Plato, as other men burned lamps before their
favorite saints, a young man fresh from a journey, *of
feature and shape seemly and beauteous, of stature
goodly and high, of flesh tender and soft, his visage
lovely and fair, his color white, intermingled with comely
reds, his eyes gray, and quick of look, his teeth white
and even, his hair yellow and abundant,* and trimmed
with more than the usual artifice of the time. It is
thus that Sir Thomas More translates the words of the
biographer of Pico, who, even in outward form and
appearance, seems an image of that inward harmony

and completeness, of which he is so perfect an example. The word *mystic* has been usually derived from a Greek word which signifies to *shut,* as if one *shut one's lips,* brooding on what cannot be uttered; but the Platonists themselves derive it rather from the act of *shutting the eyes,* that one may see the more, inwardly. Perhaps the eyes of the mystic Ficino, now long past the midway of life, had come to be thus half-closed; but when a young man, not unlike the archangel Raphael, as the Florentines of that age depicted him in his wonderful walk with Tobit, or Mercury, as he might have appeared in a painting by Sandro Botticelli or Piero di Cosimo, entered his chamber, he seems to have thought there was something not wholly earthly about him; at least, he ever afterward believed that it was not without the cooperation of the stars that the stranger had arrived on that day. For it happened that they fell into a conversation, deeper and more intimate than men usually fall into at first sight. During that conversation Ficino formed the design of devoting his remaining years to the translation of Plotinus, that new Plato, in whom the mystical element in the Platonic philosophy had been worked out to the utmost limit of vision and ecstasy; and it is in dedicating this translation to Lorenzo de' Medici that Ficino has recorded these incidents.

It was after many wanderings, wanderings of the intellect as well as physical journeys, that Pico came to rest at Florence. He was then about twenty years old, having been born in 1463. He was called Giovanni at baptism, Pico, like all his ancestors, from Picus, nephew of the Emperor Constantine, from whom they claimed to be descended, and Mirandola from the place of his birth, a little town afterward part of the duchy of Modena, of which small territory his family had long been the feudal lords. Pico was the youngest of the family, and his mother, delighting in his wonderful memory, sent him at the age of fourteen to the famous school of law at Bologna. From the first, indeed, she seems to have had a presentiment of his future fame, for, with a faith in omens characteristic of her time, she believed that a strange circumstance had happened at the time of Pico's birth—the appearance of a circular flame which suddenly vanished away, on the wall of

the chamber where she lay. He remained two years
at Bologna; and then, with an inexhaustible, unrivalled
thirst for knowledge, the strange, confused, uncritical
learning of that age, passed through the principal schools
of Italy and France, penetrating, as he thought, into
the secrets of all ancient philosophies, and many Eastern
languages. And with this flood of erudition came the
generous hope, so often disabused, of reconciling the philosophers with each other, and all alike with the Church.
At last he came to Rome. There, like some knight-
errant of philosophy, he offered to defend nine hundred bold paradoxes, drawn from the most opposite
sources, against all comers. But the pontifical court was
led to suspect the orthodoxy of some of these propo-
sitions, and even the reading of the book which contained
them was forbidden by the Pope. It was not till 1493,
that Pico was finally absolved, by a brief of Alexander
the Sixth. Ten years before that date he had arrived at
Florence; an early instance of those who, after following
the vain hope of an impossible reconciliation from system to system, have at last fallen back unsatisfied on
the simplicities of their childhood's belief.

The oration which Pico composed for the opening
of this philosophical tournament still remains; its subject is the dignity of human nature, the greatness of
man. In common with nearly all medieval speculation,
much of Pico's writing has this for its drift; and in common also with it, Pico's theory of that dignity is founded
on a misconception of the place in nature both of the
earth, and of man. For Pico the earth is the center of
the universe; and around it, as a fixed and motionless
point, the sun and moon and stars revolve, like diligent
servants or ministers. And in the midst of all is placed
man, *nodus at vinculum mundi* (the bond or copula of
the world), and the "interpreter of nature"—that famous
expression of Bacon's really belongs to Pico. *Tritum est
in scholis,* he says, *esse hominem minorem mundum, in
quo mixtum ex elementis corpus et spiritus coelestis et
plantarum anima vegetalis et brutorum sensus et ratio
et angelica mens et Dei similitudo conspicitur.* ("It is a
commonplace of the schools that man is a little world,
in which we may discern a body mingled of earthly
elements, and ethereal breath, and the vegetable life

of plants, and the senses of the lower animals, and reason, and the intelligence of angels, and a likeness to God.") A commonplace of the schools! But perhaps it had some new significance and authority, when men heard one like Pico reiterate it; and, false as its basis was, the theory had its use. For this high dignity of man, thus bringing the dust under his feet into sensible communion with the thoughts and affections of the angels, was supposed to belong to him, not as renewed by a religious system, but by his own natural right; and it was a counterpoise to the increasing tendency of medieval religion to depreciate man's nature, to sacrifice this or that element in it, to make it ashamed of itself, to keep the degrading or painful accidents of it always in view. It helped man onward to that reassertion of himself, that rehabilitation of human nature, the body, the senses, the heart, the intelligence, which the Renaissance fulfills. And yet to read a page of one of Pico's forgotten books is like a glance into one of those ancient sepulchers, upon which the wanderer in classical lands has sometimes stumbled, with the old disused ornaments and furniture of a world wholly unlike ours still fresh in them. That whole conception of nature is so different from our own. For Pico, the world is a limited place, bounded by actual crystal walls, and a material firmament; it is like a painted toy, like that map or system of the world, held, as a great target or shield, in the hands of the gray-headed father of all things, in one of the earlier frescoes of the Campo Santo at Pisa. How different from this childish dream is our own conception of nature, with its unlimited space, its innumerable suns, and the earth but a mote in the beam; how different the strange new awe and superstition with which it fills our minds! "The silence of those infinite spaces"—says Pascal, contemplating a starlight night—"the silence of those infinite spaces terrifies me." (*Le silence éternel de ces espaces infinis m'effraie.*)

He was already almost wearied out when he came to Florence. He had loved much and been beloved by women, "wandering over the crooked hills of delicious pleasure"; but their reign over him was over, and long before Savonarola's famous "bonfire of vanities," he had

destroyed those love songs in the vulgar tongue, which
would have been such a relief to us, after the scholastic
prolixity of his Latin writings. It was in another spirit
that he composed a Platonic commentary, the only work
of his in Italian which has come down to us, on the
"Song of Divine Love"—*secondo la mente ed opinione
dei Platonici*—("according to the mind and opinion of
the Platonists")—by his friend Hieronymo Beniveni, in
which, with an ambitious array of every sort of learning,
and a profusion of imagery borrowed indifferently from
the astrologers, the Cabala, and Homer, and Scripture,
and Dionysius the Areopagite, he attempts to define the
stages by which the soul passes from the earthly to the
unseen beauty. A change indeed had passed over him,
as if the chilling touch of that abstract, disembodied
beauty which the Platonists profess to long for, had
already touched him; and perhaps it was a sense of
this, coupled with that overbrightness of his, which in
the popular imagination always betokens an early death,
that made Camilla Rucellai, one of those prophetesses
whom the preaching of Savonarola had raised up in
Florence, prophesy, seeing him for the first time, that
he would depart in the time of lilies—prematurely,
that is, like the field flowers which are withered by the
scorching sun almost as soon as they have sprung up.
It was now that he wrote down those thoughts on the
religious life which Sir Thomas More turned into English, and which another English translator thought worthy
to be added to the books of the *Imitation.* "It is not
hard to know God, provided one will not force oneself
to define him" has been thought a great saying of
Joubert's. "Love God"—Pico writes to Angelo Politian—
"we rather may, than either know him, or by speech
utter him. And yet had men liefer by knowledge never
find that which they seek, than by love possess that
thing, which also without love were in vain found."

Yet he who had this fine touch for spiritual things
did not—and in this is the enduring interest of his
story—even after his conversion, forget the old gods.
He is one of the last who seriously and sincerely entertained the claims on men's faith of the pagan religions; he is anxious to ascertain the true significance
of the obscurest legend, the lightest tradition concern-

ing them. With many thoughts and many influences which led him in that direction, he did not become a monk; only he became gentle and patient in disputation; retaining "somewhat of the old plenty, in dainty viand and silver vessel," he gave over the greater part of his property to his friend, the mystical poet Beniveni, to be spent by him in works of charity, chiefly in the sweet charity of providing marriage doweries for the peasant girls of Florence. His end came in 1494, when, amid the prayers and sacraments of Savonarola, he died of fever, on the very day on which Charles the Eighth entered Florence, the seventeenth of November, yet in the time of lilies, the lilies of the shield of France, as the people now said, remembering Camilla's prophecy. He was buried in the cloister at Saint Mark's, in the hood and white frock of the Dominican order.

It is became the life of Pico, thus lying down to rest in the Dominican habit, yet amid thoughts of the older gods, himself like one of those comely divinities, reconciled indeed to the new religion, but still with a tenderness for the earlier life, and desirous literally to "bind the ages each to each by natural piety"—it is because this life is so perfect a parallel to the attempt made in his writings to reconcile Christianity with the ideas of paganism, that Pico, in spite of the scholastic character of those writings, is really interesting. Thus, in the *Heptaplus, or Discourse on the Seven Days of the Creation,* he endeavors to reconcile the accounts which pagan philosophy had given of the origin of the world with the account given in the books of Moses—the *Timaeus* of Plato with the book of *Genesis.* The *Heptaplus* is dedicated to Lorenzo the Magnificent, whose interest, the preface tells us, in the secret wisdom of Moses is well known. If Moses seems in his writings simple and even popular, rather than either a philosopher or a theologian, that is because it was an institution with the ancient philosophers, either not to speak of divine things at all, or to speak of them dissemblingly; hence their doctrines were called mysteries. Taught by them, Pythagoras became so great a "master of silence," and wrote almost nothing, thus hiding the words of God in his heart, and speaking wisdom only among the perfect. In explaining the harmony between Plato and

Moses, Pico lays hold on every sort of figure and analogy, on the double meanings of words, the symbols of the Jewish ritual, the secondary meanings of obscure stories in the later Greek mythologists. Everywhere there is an unbroken system of correspondences. Every object in the material world is an analogue, a symbol or counterpart, of some higher reality in the starry heavens, and this again of some law of the angelic life in the world beyond the stars. There is the element of fire in the material world; the sun is the fire of heaven; and there is, in the supercelestial world, the fire of the seraphic intelligence. "But behold how they differ! The elementary fire burns, the heavenly fire vivifies, the supercelestial fire loves." In this way, every natural object, every combination of natural forces, every accident in the lives of men, is filled with higher meanings. Omens, prophecies, supernatural coincidences, accompany Pico himself all through life. There are oracles in every tree and mountaintop, and a significance in every accidental combination of the events of life.

This constant tendency to symbolism and imagery gives Pico's work a figured style, by which it has some real resemblance to Plato's, and he differs from other mystical writers of his time by a real desire to know his authorities at first hand. He reads Plato in Greek, Moses in Hebrew, and by this his work really belongs to the higher culture. Above all, there is a constant sense in reading him, that his thoughts, however little their positive value may be, are connected with springs beneath them of deep and passionate emotion; and when he explains the grades or steps by which the soul passes from the love of a physical object to the love of unseen beauty, and unfolds the analogies between this process and other movements upward of human thought, there is a glow and vehemence in his words, which remind one of the manner in which his own brief existence flamed itself away.

I said that the Renaissance of the fifteenth century was in many things great, rather by what it designed or aspired to do, than by what it actually achieved. It remained for a later age to conceive the true method of effecting a scientific reconciliation of Christian sentiment with the imagery, the legends, the theories about the world, of pagan poetry and philosophy. For that age the only possible reconciliation was an imaginative one, and resulted from the efforts of artists, trained in Christian schools, to handle pagan subjects; and of this artistic reconciliation work like Pico's was but the feebler counterpart. Whatever philosophers had to say on one side or the other, whether they were successful or not in their attempts to reconcile the old to the new, and to justify the expènditure of so much care and thought on the dreams of a dead religion, the imagery of the Greek religion, the direct charm of its story, were by artists valued and cultivated for their own sake. Hence, a new sort of mythology, with a tone and qualities of its own. When the shipload of sacred earth from the soil of Jerusalem was mingled with the common clay in the Campo Santo at Pisa, a new flower grew up from it, unlike any flower men had seen before, the anemone with its concentric rings of strangely blended color, still to be found by those who search long enough for it, in the long grass of the Maremma. Just such a strange flower was that mythology of the Italian Renaissance, which grew up from the mixture of two traditions, two sentiments, the sacred and the profane. Classical story was regarded as a mere datum to be received and assimilated. It did not come into men's minds to ask curiously of science concerning its origin, its primary form and import, its meaning for those who projected it. It sank into their minds, to issue forth again with all the tangle about it of medieval sentiments and ideas. In the *Doni* Madonna in the Tribune of the Uffizi, Michelangelo actually brings the pagan religion, and with it the unveiled human form, the sleepy-looking fauns of a Dionysiac revel, into the presence of the Madonna, as simpler painters had introduced other products of the earth, birds or flowers; and he has given to that Madonna herself much of the uncouth energy of the older and more primitive mighty Mother.

It is because this picturesque union of contrasts, belonging properly to the art of the close of the fifteenth century, pervades, in Pico della Mirandola, an actual person, that the figure of Pico is so attractive. He will not let one go; he wins one on, in spite of oneself, to turn again to the pages of his forgotten books, although we know already that the actual solution proposed in them will satisfy us as little as perhaps it satisfied him. It is said that in his eagerness for mysterious learning he once paid a great sum for a collection of cabalistic manuscripts, which turned out to be forgeries; and the story might well stand as a parable of all he ever seemed to gain in the way of actual knowledge. He had sought knowledge, and passed from system to system, and hazarded much; but less for the sake of positive knowledge than because he believed there was a spirit of order and beauty in knowledge, which would come down and unite what men's ignorance had divided, and renew what time had made dim. And so, while his actual work has passed away, yet his own qualities are still active, and he himself remains, as one alive in the grave, *caesiis et vigilibus oculis,* as his biographer describes him, and with that sanguine, clear skin, *decenti rubore interspersa,* as with the light of morning upon it; and he has a true place in that group of great Italians who fill the end of the fifteenth century with their names—he is a true *humanist.* For the essence of humanism is that belief of which he seems never to have doubted, that nothing which has ever interested living men and women can wholly lose its vitality—no language they have spoken, nor oracle beside which they have hushed their voices, no dream which has once been entertained by actual human minds, nothing about which they have ever been passionate, or expended time and zeal.

SANDRO BOTTICELLI

IN Leonardo's treatise on painting only one contemporary is mentioned by name—Sandro Botticelli. This pre-eminence may be due to chance only, but to some will rather appear a result of deliberate judgment; for people have begun to find out the charm of Botticelli's work, and his name, little known in the last century, is quietly becoming important. In the middle of the fifteenth century he had already anticipated much of that meditative subtlety, which is sometimes supposed peculiar to the great imaginative workmen of its close. Leaving the simple religion which had occupied the followers of Giotto for a century, and the simple naturalism which had grown out of it, a thing of birds and flowers only, he sought inspiration in what to him were works of the modern world, the writings of Dante and Boccaccio, and in new readings of his own of classical stories; or, if he painted religious incidents, painted them with an undercurrent of original sentiment, which touches you as the real matter of the picture through the veil of its ostensible subject. What is the peculiar sensation, what is the peculiar quality of pleasure, which his work has the property of exciting in us, and which we cannot get elsewhere? For this, especially when he has to speak of a comparatively unknown artist, is always the chief question which a critic has to answer.

In an age when the lives of artists were full of adventure, his life is almost colorless. Criticism indeed has cleared away much of the gossip which Vasari accumulated, has touched the legend of Lippo and Lucrezia, and rehabilitated the character of Andrea del Castagno; but in Botticelli's case there is no legend to dissipate. He did not even go by his true name: Sandro is a nickname, and his true name is Filipepi, Botticelli being only the name of the goldsmith who first taught him art. Only two things happened to him, two things which he shared with other artists—he was invited to Rome to paint in the Sistine Chapel, and he fell in later life under the influence of Savonarola, passing apparently almost out of men's sight in a sort of religious melancholy, which lasted till his death in 1515, according to the received date. Vasari says that he plunged into the study of Dante, and even wrote a comment on the *Divine Comedy*. But it seems strange that he should have lived on inactive so long; and one almost wishes that some document might come to light, which, fixing the date of his death earlier, might relieve one, in thinking of him, of his dejected old age.

He is before all things a poetical painter, blending the charm of story and sentiment, the medium of the art of poetry, with the charm of line and color, the medium of abstract painting. So he becomes the illustrator of Dante. In a few rare examples of the edition of 1481, the blank spaces, left at the beginning of every canto for the hand of the illuminator, have been filled, as far as the nineteenth canto of the *Inferno,* with impressions of engraved plates,

seemingly by way of experiment, for in the copy in the
Bodleian Library, one of the three impressions it contains
has been printed upside down, and much awry, in the
midst of the luxurious printed page. Giotto, and the followers of Giotto, with their almost childish religious aim,
had not learned to put that weight of meaning into outward things, light, color, everyday gesture, which the
poetry of the *Divine Comedy* involves, and before the
fifteenth century Dante could hardly have found an illustrator. Botticelli's illustrations are crowded with incident,
blending, with a naive carelessness of pictorial propriety,
three phases of the same scene into one plate. The grotesques, so often a stumbling block to painters who forget
that the words of a poet, which only feebly present an
image to the mind, must be lowered in key when translated into form, make one regret that he has not rather
chosen for illustration the more subdued imagery of the
Purgatorio. Yet in the scene of those who "go down quick
into hell," there is an invention about the fire taking hold
on the upturned soles of the feet, which proves that the
design is no mere translation of Dante's words, but a
true painter's vision; while the scene of the Centaurs wins
one at once, for forgetful of the actual circumstances of
their appearance, Botticelli has gone off with delight on
the thought of the Centaurs themselves, bright, small
creatures of the woodland, with arch baby faces and
mignon forms, drawing tiny bows.

Botticelli lived in a generation of naturalists, and he
might have been a mere naturalist among them. There
are traces enough in his work of that alert sense of outward things, which, in the pictures of that period, fills
the lawns with delicate living creatures, and the hillsides
with pools of water, and the pools of water with flowering
reeds. But this was not enough for him; he is a visionary
painter, and in his visionariness he resembles Dante.
Giotto, the tried companion of Dante, Masaccio, Ghirlandaio even, do but transcribe, with more or less refining, the
outward image; they are dramatic, not visionary painters;
they are almost impassive spectators of the action before
them. But the genius of which Botticelli is the type usurps
the data before it as the exponent of ideas, moods, visions
of its own; in this interest it plays fast and loose with
those data, rejecting some and isolating others, and al-

ways combining them anew. To him, as to Dante, the scene, the color, the outward image or gesture, comes with all its incisive and importunate reality; but awakes in him, moreover, through some subtle structure of his own, a mood which it awakes in no one else, of which it is the double or repetition, and which it clothes, that all may share it, with sensuous circumstances.

But he is far enough from accepting the conventional orthodoxy of Dante which, referring all human action to the easy formula of purgatory, heaven and hell, leaves an insoluble element of prose in the depths of Dante's poetry. One picture of his, with the portrait of the donor, Matteo Palmieri, below, had the credit or discredit of attracting some shadow of ecclesiastical censure. This Matteo Palmieri—two dim figures move under that name in contemporary history—was the reputed author of a poem, still unedited, La Città Divina, which represented the human race as an incarnation of those angels who, in the revolt of Lucifer, were neither for Jehovah nor for his enemies, a fantasy of that earlier Alexandrian philosophy, about which the Florentine intellect in that century was so curious. Botticelli's picture may have been only one of those familiar compositions in which religious reverie has recorded its impressions of the various forms of beatified existence—Glorias, as they were called, like that in which Giotto painted the portrait of Dante; but somehow it was suspected of embodying in a picture the wayward dream of Palmieri, and the chapel where it hung was closed. Artists so entire as Botticelli are usually careless about philosophical theories, even when the philosopher is a Florentine of the fifteenth century, and his work a poem in terza rima. But Botticelli, who wrote a commentary on Dante, and became the disciple of Savonarola, may well have let such theories come and go across him. True or false, the story interprets much of the peculiar sentiment with which he infuses his profane and sacred persons, comely, and in a certain sense like angels, but with a sense of displacement or loss about them—the wistfulness of exiles, conscious of a passion and energy greater than any known issue of them explains, which runs through all his varied work with a sentiment of ineffable melancholy.

So just what Dante scorns as unworthy alike of heaven

and hell, Botticelli accepts, that middle world in which
men take no side in great conflicts, and decide no great
causes, and make great refusals. He thus sets for himself
the limits within which art, undisturbed by any moral
ambition, does its most sincere and surest work. His interest is neither in the untempered goodness of Angelico's
saints, nor the untempered evil of Orcagna's *Inferno;* but
with men and women, in their mixed and uncertain condition, always attractive, clothed sometimes by passion
with a character of loveliness and energy, but saddened
perpetually by the shadow upon them of the great things
from which they shrink. His morality is all sympathy;
and it is this sympathy, conveying into his work somewhat more than is usual of the true complexion of humanity, which makes him, visionary as he is, so forcible
a realist.

It is this which gives to his Madonnas their unique
expression and charm. He has worked out in them a
distinct and peculiar type, definite enough in his own
mind, for he has painted it over and over again, sometimes one might think almost mechanically, as a pastime
during that dark period when his thoughts were so heavy
upon him. Hardly any collection of note is without one
of these circular pictures, into which the attendant angels
depress their heads so naively. Perhaps you have sometimes wondered why those peevish-looking Madonnas,
conformed to no acknowledged or obvious type of beauty,
attract you more and more, and often come back to you
when the Sistine Madonna and the Virgins of Fra Angelico are forgotten. At first, contrasting them with those,
you may have thought that there was even something in
them mean or abject, for the abstract lines of the face
have little nobleness, and the color is wan. For with
Botticelli she too, though she holds in her hands the
"desire of all nations," is one of those who are neither
for Jehovah nor for his enemies; and her choice is on her
face. The white light on it is cast up hard and cheerless
from below, as when snow lies upon the ground, and the
children look up with surprise at the strange whiteness
of the ceiling. Her trouble is in the very caress of the
mysterious child, whose gaze is always far from her, and
who has already that sweet look of devotion which men
have never been able altogether to love, and which still

makes the born saint an object almost of suspicion to
his earthly brethren. Once, indeed, he guides her hand to
transcribe in a book the words of her exaltation, the *Ave,*
and the *Magnificat,* and the *Gaude Maria,* and the young
angels, glad to rouse her for a moment from her dejection, are eager to hold the inkhorn and to support the
book; but the pen almost drops from her hand, and the
high cold words have no meaning for her, and her true
children are those others, in the midst of whom, in her
rude home, the intolerable honor came to her, with that
look of wistful inquiry on their irregular faces which you
see in startled animals—gipsy children, such as those who,
in Apennine villages, still hold out their long brown arms
to beg of you, but on Sundays become *enfants du chœur,*
with their thick black hair nicely combed, and fair white
linen on their sun-burnt throats.

What is strangest is that he carries this sentiment into
classical subjects, its most complete expression being a
picture in the Uffizi, of Venus rising from the sea, in
which the grotesque emblems of the Middle Ages, and a
landscape full of its peculiar feeling, and even its strange
draperies, powdered all over in the Gothic manner with
a quaint conceit of daisies, frame a figure that reminds
you of the faultless nude studies of Ingres. At first, perhaps, you are attracted only by a quaintness of design,
which seems to recall all at once whatever you have read
of Florence in the fifteenth century; afterward you may
think that this quaintness must be incongruous with the
subject, and that the color is cadaverous or at least cold.
And yet, the more you come to understand what imaginative coloring really is, that all color is no mere delightful
quality of natural things, but a spirit upon them by which
they become expressive to the spirit, the better you will
like this peculiar quality of color, and you will find
that quaint design of Botticelli's a more direct inlet into
the Greek temper than the works of the Greeks themselves even of the finest period. Of the Greeks as they
really were, of their difference from ourselves, of the
aspects of their outward life, we know far more than
Botticelli, or his most learned contemporaries; but for us,
long familiarity has taken off the edge of the lesson, and
we are hardly conscious of what we owe to the Hellenic
spirit. But in pictures like this of Botticelli's you have

a record of the first impression made by it on minds
turned back toward it, in almost painful aspiration, from
a world in which it had been ignored so long; and in the
passion, the energy, the industry of realization, with which
Botticelli carries out his intention, is the exact measure
of the legitimate influence over the human mind of the
imaginative system of which this is the central myth. The
light is indeed cold—mere sunless dawn; but a later
painter would have cloyed you with sunshine; and you can
see the better for that quietness in the morning air each
long promontory, as it slopes down to the water's edge.
Men go forth to their labors until the evening; but she
is awake before them, and you might think that the sorrow in her face was at the thought of the whole long day
of love yet to come. An emblematical figure of the wind
blows hard across the gray water, moving forward the
dainty-lipped shell on which she sails, the sea "showing
his teeth" as it moves in thin lines of foam, and sucking
in, one by one, the falling roses, each severe in outline,
plucked off short at the stalk, but embrowned a little, as
Botticelli's flowers always are. Botticelli meant all that imagery to be altogether pleasurable; and it was partly an incompleteness of resources, inseparable from the art of that
time, that subdued and chilled it; but his predilection for
minor tones counts also; and what is unmistakable is the
sadness with which he has conceived the goddess of pleasure, as the depositary of a great power over the lives of
men.

I have said that the peculiar character of Botticelli is the
result of a blending in him of a sympathy for humanity in
its uncertain condition, its attractiveness, its investiture at
rarer moments in a character of loveliness and energy,
with his consciousness of the shadow upon it of the great
things from which it shrinks, and that this conveys into his
work somewhat more than painting usually attains of the
true complexion of humanity. He paints the story of the
goddess of pleasure in other episodes besides that of her
birth from the sea, but never without some shadow of death
in the gray flesh and wan flowers. He paints Madonnas,
but they shrink from the pressure of the divine child, and
plead in unmistakable undertones for a warmer, lower
humanity. The same figure—tradition connects it with
Simonetta, the mistress of Giuliano de' Medici—appears

again as Judith, returning home across the hill country, when the great deed is over, and the moment of revulsion come, and the olive branch in her hand is becoming a burden; as *Justice,* sitting on a throne, but with a fixed look of self-hatred which makes the sword in her hand seem that of a suicide; and again as *Veritas,* in the allegorical picture of *Calumnia,* where one may note in passing the suggestiveness of an accident which identifies the image of Truth with the person of Venus. We might trace the same sentiment through his engravings; but his share in them is doubtful, and the object of this fragment has been attained, if I have defined aright the temper in which he worked.

But, after all, it may be asked, is a painter like Botticelli —a secondary painter, a proper subject for general criticism? There are a few great painters, like Michelangelo or Leonardo, whose work has become a force in general culture, partly for this very reason that they have absorbed into themselves all such workmen as Sandro Botticelli; and, over and above mere technical or antiquarian criticism, general criticism may be very well employed in that sort of interpretation which adjusts the position of these men to general culture, whereas smaller men can be the proper subjects only of technical or antiquarian treatment. But, besides those great men, there is a certain number of artists who have a distinct faculty of their own by which they convey to us a peculiar quality of pleasure which we cannot get elsewhere; and these, too, have their place in general culture, and have to be interpreted to it by those who have felt their charm strongly, and are often the objects of a special diligence and a consideration wholly affectionate, just because there is not about them the stress of a great name and authority. Of this select number Botticelli is one; he has the freshness, the uncertain and diffident promise which belongs to the earlier Renaissance itself, and makes it perhaps the most interesting period in the history of the mind; in studying his work one begins to understand to how great a place in human culture the art of Italy had been called.

LUCA DELLA ROBBIA

THE Italian sculptors of the earlier half of the fifteenth century are more than mere forerunners of the great masters of its close, and often reach perfection, within the narrow limits which they chose to impose on their work. Their sculpture shares with the paintings of Botticelli and the churches of Brunelleschi that profound expressiveness, that intimate impress of an indwelling soul, which is the peculiar fascination of the art of Italy in that century. Their works have been much neglected, and often almost hidden away amid the frippery of modern decoration, and we come with some surprise on the places where their fire still smolders. One longs to penetrate into the lives of the men who have given expression to so much power and sweetness; but it is part of the reserve, the austere dignity and simplicity of their existence, that their histories are for the most part lost, or told but briefly: from their lives, as from their work, all tumult of sound and color has passed away. Mino, the Raphael of sculpture, Maso del Rodario, whose works add a new grace to the church of Como, Donatello even—one asks in vain for more than a shadowy outline of their actual days.

Something more remains of Luca della Robbia; something more of a history, of outward changes and fortunes, is expressed through his work. I suppose nothing brings the real air of a Tuscan town so vividly to mind as those pieces of pale blue and white earthenware, by which he is best known, like fragments of the milky sky itself, fallen into the cool streets, and breaking into the darkened churches. And no work is less imitable: like Tuscan wine, it loses its savor when moved from its birthplace, from the crumbling walls where it was first placed. Part of the charm of this work, its grace, and purity, and finish of expression, is common to all the Tuscan sculptors of the fifteenth century; for Luca was first of all a worker in marble, and his works in earthenware only transfer to a different material the principles of his sculpture.

These Tuscan sculptors of the fifteenth century worked for the most part in low relief, giving even to their monumental effigies something of its depression of surface, getting into them by this means a touching suggestion of the wasting and etherealization of death. They are haters of all heaviness and emphasis, of strongly opposed light and shade, and look for their means of expression among the last refinements of shadow, which are almost invisible except in a strong light, and which the finest pencil can hardly follow. The whole essence of their work is expression, the passing of a smile over the face of a child, the ripple of the air on a still day over the curtain of a window ajar.

What is the precise value of this system of sculpture, this low relief? Luca della Robbia, and the other sculptors of the school to which he belongs, have before them the universal problem of their art; and this system of low relief is the means by which they meet and overcome the special limitation of sculpture, a limitation which results from the material, and the essential conditions, of all sculptured work, and which consists in the tendency of this work to a hard realism, a one-sided presentment of mere form, that solid material frame which only motion can relieve, a thing of heavy shadows and an individuality of expression pushed to caricature. Against this tendency to a hard presentment of mere form which tries vainly to compete with the reality of nature itself, all noble sculpture is constantly struggling: each great system of sculpture resisting it in its own way, etherealizing, spiritualizing, relieving its hardness, its heaviness and death. The use of color in sculpture is but an unskillful contrivance to effect, by borrowing from another art, what the nobler sculpture effects by strictly appropriate means. To get not color, but the equivalent of color, to secure the expression and the play of life; to expand the too fixed individuality of pure, unrelieved, uncolored form —this is the problem which the three great styles in sculpture have solved in three different ways.

Allgemeinheit—breadth, generality, universality—is the word chosen by Winckelmann, and after him by Goethe and many German critics, to express that law of the most excellent Greek sculptors, of Phidias and his pupils, which prompted them constantly to seek the type in the individual, to purge from the individual all that belongs only to the individual, all the accidents, feelings, actions of a special moment, all that, in its own nature enduring but for a moment, looks like a frozen thing if you arrest it, to abstract and express only what is structural, and permanent.

In this way their works came to be like some subtle extract or essence, or almost like pure thoughts or ideas; and hence that broad humanity in them, that detachment from the conditions of a particular place or people, which has carried their influence far beyond the age which produced them, and insured them universal acceptance.

That was the Greek way of relieving the hardness and unspirituality of pure form. But it involved to a certain degree the sacrifice of what we call *expression;* and a system of abstraction which aimed always at the broad and general type, at the purging away from the individual of what belonged only to him, and of the mere accidents of a particular time and place, imposed upon the range of effects open to the Greek sculptor limits strictly defined; and when Michelangelo came, with a genius spiritualized by the reverie of the Middle Ages, penetrated by its spirit of inwardness and introspection, living not a mere outward life like the Greek, but a life full of inward experiences, sorrows, consolations, a system which sacrificed what was inward could not satisfy him. To him, lover and student of Greek sculpture as he was, work which did not bring what was inward to the surface, which was not concerned with individual expression, character, feeling, the special history of the special soul, was not worth doing at all.

And so, in a way quite personal and peculiar to himself, which often is, and always seems, the effect of accident, he secured for his work individuality and intensity of expression, while he avoided a too hard realism, that tendency which the representation of feeling in sculpture always has to harden into caricature. What time and accident, its centuries of darkness, under the furrows of the "little Melian farm," has done with a singular felicity of touch for the Venus of Melos, fraying its surface and softening its lines, so that some spirit in the thing seems always on the point of breaking out of it, as if in it classical sculpture had advanced already one step into the mystical Christian age, so that of all ancient work its effect is most like that of Michelangelo's own work—this effect Michelangelo gains by leaving nearly all his sculpture in a puzzling sort of incompleteness, which suggests rather than realizes actual form. Something of the wasting of that snow image which he molded at the command of Piero de' Medici, when the snow lay one night in the court of the Pitti palace, almost always lurks about it, as if he had determined to make the quality of a task, exacted from him half in derision, the pride of all his work. Many have wondered at that incompleteness, suspecting however that Michelangelo himself loved and was loath to change it, and feeling at the same time that they too would lose something if that half-realized form ever quite emerged from the stone, so rough-hewn here, so delicately finished there; and they have wished to fathom the charm of this incompleteness. Well! that incompleteness is Michelangelo's equivalent for color in sculpture; it is his way of etherealizing pure form, of relieving its hard realism, and communicating to it breath, pulsation, the effect of life. It was a characteristic too which fell in with his peculiar temper and mode of life, his disappointments and hesitations. And it was in reality perfect finish. In this way he combines the utmost amount of passion and intensity with the sense of a yielding and flexible life: he gets not vitality merely, but a wonderful force of expression.

Midway between these two systems—the system of the Greek sculptors and the system of Michelangelo—comes the system of Luca della Robbia and the other Tuscan sculptors of the fifteenth century, partaking both of the *Allgemeinheit* of the Greeks, their way of extracting certain select elements only of pure form, and sacrificing all the rest, and the studied incompleteness of Michelangelo, relieving that expression of intensity, passion, energy, which would otherwise have hardened into caricature. Like Michelangelo, these sculptors fill their works with intense and individualized expression: their noblest works are the studied sepulchral portraits of particular persons—the monument of Conte Ugo in the Badía of Florence, of the youthful Medea Colleoni, with the wonderful, long throat, in the chapel on the cool north side of the Church of Santa Maria Maggiore at Bergamo—and they unite the element of tranquillity, of repose, to this intense and individualized expression, by a system of conventionalism as subtle and skillful as that of the Greeks, by subduing all the curves which indicate solid form, and throwing the whole into lower relief.

The life of Luca, a life of labor and frugality, with no

adventure, and no excitement, except what belongs to the
trial of new artistic processes, the struggle with new artistic
difficulties, the solution of purely artistic problems, fills the
first seventy years of the fifteenth century. After producing
many works in marble for the Duomo and the Campanile
of Florence, which place him among the foremost sculptors
of that age, he became desirous to realize the spirit, the
manner of that sculpture, in a humbler material, to unite
its science, its exquisite and expressive system of low
relief, to the homely art of pottery, to introduce those high
qualities into common things, to adorn and cultivate daily
household life. In this he is profoundly characteristic of
the Florence of that century, of that in it which lay below
its superficial vanity and caprice, a certain old-world
modesty and seriousness and simplicity. People had not yet
begun to think that what was good art for churches was
not so good, or less fitted, for their own houses. Luca's
new work was of plain white at first, a mere rough imitation
of the costly, laboriously wrought marble, finished in a few
hours. But on this humble path he found his way to a
fresh success, to another artistic grace. The fame of oriental pottery, with its strange, bright colors—colors of art,
colors not to be attained in the natural stone—mingled
with the tradition of the old Roman pottery of the neighborhood. The little red, coral-like jars of Arezzo, dug up
in that district from time to time, are still famous. These
colors haunted Luca's fancy. "He still continued seeking
something more," his biographer says of him, "and instead
of making his figures of baked earth simply white, he
added the further invention of giving them color, to the
astonishment and delight of all who beheld them"—*Cosa
singolare, e multo utile per la state!*—a curious thing, and
very useful for summertime, full of coolness and repose
for hand and eye. Luca loved the forms of various fruits,
and wrought them into all sorts of marvelous frames and
garlands, giving them their natural colors, only subdued a
little, a little paler than nature. But in his nobler terra
cottas, he never introduces color into the flesh, keeping
mostly to blue and white, the colors of the Virgin Mary.

I said that the work of Luca della Robbia possessed in
an unusual measure that special characteristic which belongs to all the workmen of his school, a characteristic
which, even in the absence of much positive information

about their actual history, seems to bring the workman himself very near to us, the impress of a personal quality, a profound expressiveness, what the French call *intimité*, by which is meant a subtler sense of originality, the seal on a man's work of what is most inward and peculiar in his moods, and manner of apprehension: it is what we call expression, carried to its highest intensity of degree. That characteristic is rare in poetry, rarer still in art, rarest of all in the abstract art of sculpture; yet essentially, perhaps, is the quality which alone makes works in the imaginative and moral order really worth having at all. It is because the works of the artists of the fifteenth century possess this quality in an unmistakable way that one is anxious to know all that can be known about them, and explain to oneself the secret of their charm.

THE POETRY OF MICHELANGELO

CRITICS of Michelangelo have sometimes spoken as if the only characteristic of his genius were a wonderful strength, verging, as in the things of the imagination great strength always does, on what is singular or strange. A certain strangeness, something of the blossoming of the aloe, is indeed an element in all true works of art; that they shall excite or surprise us is indispensable. But that they shall give pleasure and exert a charm over us is indispensable too; and this strangeness must be sweet also, a lovely strangeness. And to the true admirers of Michelangelo this is the true type of the Michelangelesque— sweetness and strength, pleasure with surprise, an energy of conception which seems at every moment about to break through all the conditions of comely form, recovering, touch by touch, a loveliness found usually only in the simplest natural things—*ex forti dulcedo*.

In this way he sums up for them the whole character of medieval art itself, in that which distinguishes it most clearly from classical work, the presence of a convulsive energy in it, becoming in lower hands merely monstrous or forbidding, but felt, even in its most graceful products, as a subdued quaintness or grotesque. Yet those who feel this grace or sweetness in Michelangelo might at the first moment be puzzled if they were asked wherein precisely the quality resided. Men of inventive temperament—Victor Hugo, for instance, in whom, as in Michelangelo, people have for the most part been attracted or repelled by the strength, while few have understood his sweetness—have sometimes relieved conceptions of merely moral or spiritual greatness, but with little aesthetic charm of their own, by lovely accidents, or accessories, like the butterfly which alights on the blood-stained barricade in *Les Misérables,* or those sea birds for whom the monstrous Gilliatt comes to be as some wild natural thing, so that they are no longer afraid of him, in *Les Travailleurs de la Mer.* But the austere genius of Michelangelo will not depend for its sweetness on any mere accessories like these. The world of natural things has almost no existence for him; "When one speaks of him," says Grimm, "woods, clouds, seas, and mountains disappear, and only what is formed by the spirit of man remains behind"; and he quotes a few slight words from a letter of his to Vasari, as the single expression in all he has left of a feeling for nature. He has traced no flowers, like those with which Leonardo stars over his gloomiest rocks; nothing like the fretwork of wings and flames in which Blake frames his most startling conceptions; no forest scenery like Titian's fills his backgrounds, but only blank ranges of rock, and dim vegetable forms as blank as they, as in a world before the creation of the first five days.

Of the whole story of the creation he has painted only the creation of the first man and woman, and, for him at least, feebly, the creation of light. It belongs to the quality of his genius thus to concern itself almost exclusively with the creation of man. For him it is not, as in the story itself, the last and crowning act of a series of developments, but the first and unique act, the creation of life itself in its supreme form, offhand and immediately, in the cold and lifeless stone. With him the beginning of life has all the characteristics of resurrection; it is like the recovery of suspended health or animation, with its gratitude, its effusion, and eloquence. Fair as the young men of the Elgin marbles, the Adam of the Sistine Chapel is unlike them in a total absence of that balance and completeness, which express so well the sentiment of a self-contained, independent life. In that languid figure there is something rude and satyrlike, something akin to the rugged hillside on which it lies. His whole form is gathered into an expression of mere expectation and reception; he has hardly strength enough to lift his finger to touch the finger of the creator; yet a touch of the fingertips will suffice.

This creation of life, life coming always as relief or recovery, and always in strong contrast with the rough-hewn mass in which it is kindled, is in various ways the motive of all his work, whether its immediate subject be pagan or Christian, legend or allegory; and this, although at least one half of his work was designed for the adornment of tombs—the tomb of Julius, the tombs of the Medici. Not the Judgment but the Resurrection is the real subject of his last work in the Sistine Chapel; and his favorite pagan subject is the legend of Leda, the delight of the world breaking from the egg of a bird. He secures that ideality of expression, which in Greek sculpture depends on a delicate system of abstraction, and in early Italian sculpture on lowness of relief, by an incompleteness, which is surely not always undesigned, and which I suppose no one regrets, and trusts to the spectator to complete the half-emergent form. And as his persons have something of the unwrought stone about them, so, as if to realize the expression by which the old Florentine records describe a sculptor—*master of live stone*—with him the very rocks seem to have life; they have but to cast away the dust and scurf that they may rise and stand on their feet. He loved the very quarries of Carrara, those strange gray peaks which even at midday convey into any scene from which they are visible, something of the solemnity and stillness of evening, sometimes wandering among them month after month, till at last their pale ashen colors seem to have passed into his painting; and on the crown of the head of the *David* there still remains a morsel of uncut stone, as if by one touch to maintain its connection with the place from which it was hewn.

And it is in this penetrative suggestion of life that the secret of that sweetness of his is to be found. He gives us indeed no lovely natural objects like Leonardo, or Titian, but only the coldest, most elementary shadowing of rock or tree; no lovely draperies and comely gestures of life, but only the austere truths of human nature; "simple persons"—as he replied in his rough way to the querulous criticism of Julius the Second, that there was no gold on the figures of the Sistine Chapel—"simple persons, who wore no gold on their garments"; but he penetrates us with a sense of that power which we associate with all the warmth and fullness of the world, and the sense of which brings into one's thoughts a swarm of birds and flowers and insects. The brooding spirit of life itself is there; and the summer may burst out in a moment.

He was born in an interval of a rapid midnight journey in March, at a place in the neighborhood of Arezzo, the thin, clear air of which it was then thought was favorable to the birth of children of great parts. He came of a race of grave and dignified men, who, claiming kinship with the family of Canossa, and some color of imperial blood in their veins, had, generation after generation, received honorable employment under the government of Florence. His mother, a girl of nineteen years, put him out to nurse at a country house among the hills of Settignano, where every other inhabitant is a worker in the marble quarries, and the child early became familiar with that strange first stage in the sculptor's art. To this succeeded the influence of the sweetest and most placid master Florence had yet seen, Domenico Ghirlandaio. At fifteen he was at work among the curiosities of the garden of the Medici, copying and restoring antiques, winning the condescending notice of the great Lorenzo. He knew too how to excite strong hatreds; and it was at this time that in a quarrel with a fellow student he received a blow on the face, which deprived him for ever of the dignity of outward form. It was through an accident that he came to study those works of the early Italian sculptors which suggested much of his own grandest work, and impressed it with so deep a sweetness. He believed in dreams and omens. One of his friends dreamed twice that Lorenzo, then lately dead, appeared to him in gray and dusty apparel. To Michelangelo this dream seemed to portend the troubles which afterward really came, and with the suddenness which was characteristic of all his movements, he left Florence. Having occasion to pass through Bologna, he neglected to procure the little seal of red wax which the stranger entering Bologna must carry on the thumb of his right hand. He had no money to pay the fine, and would have been thrown into prison, had not one of the magistrates interposed. He remained in this man's house a whole year, rewarding his hospitality by readings from the Italian poets whom he loved. Bologna, with its endless colonnades, and fantastic leaning towers, can never have been one of the lovelier cities of Italy. But about the portals of its vast unfinished churches, and its dark shrines, half-hidden by votive flowers and candles, lie some of the sweetest works of the early Tuscan sculptors, Giovanni da Pisa and Jacopo della Quercia, things as soft as flowers, and the year which Michelangelo spent in copying these works was not a lost year. It was now, on returning to Florence, that he put forth that unique conception of Bacchus, which expresses, not the mirthfulness of the god of wine, but his sleepy seriousness, his enthusiasm, his capacity for profound dreaming. No one ever expressed more truly than Michelangelo the notion of inspired sleep, of faces charged with dreams. A vast fragment of marble had long lain below the Loggia of Orcagna, and many a sculptor had had his thoughts of a design which should just fill this famous block of stone, cutting the diamond, as it were, without loss. Under Michelangelo's hand it became the *David,* which stood till lately on the steps of the Palazzo Vecchio, when it was replaced below the Loggia. Michelangelo was now thirty years old, and his reputation was established. Three great works fill the remainder of his life; three works often interrupted, carried on through a thousand hesitations, a thousand disappointments, quarrels with his patrons, quarrels with his family, quarrels perhaps most of all with himself—the Sistine Chapel, the Mausoleum of Julius the Second, and the sacristy of San Lorenzo.

In the story of Michelangelo's life, the strength, often turning to bitterness, is not far to seek; a discordant note sounds throughout it, which almost spoils the music. He "treats the Pope as the King of France himself would not dare to treat him"; he goes along the streets of Rome "like an executioner," Raphael says of him. Once, he seems to have shut himself up with the intention of starving himself to death. As one comes in reading his life on its harsh, untempered incidents, the thought again and again arises that he is one of those who incur the judgment of Dante, as having *willfully lived in sadness.* Even his tenderness and pity are embittered by their strength. What passionate weeping in that mysterious figure which, in the *Creation of*

Adam, crouches below the image of the Almighty, as he comes with the forms of things to be, woman and her progeny, in the fold of his garment! What a sense of wrong in those two captive youths, who feel the chains like scalding water, on their proud and delicate flesh! The idealist who became a reformer with Savonarola, and a republican superintending the fortification of Florence—the nest where he was born, *il nido ove naqqu'io,* as he calls it once, in a sudden throb of affection—in its last struggle for liberty, yet believed always that he had imperial blood in his veins, and was of the kindred of the great Matilda, had within the depths of his nature some secret spring of indignation or sorrow. We know little of his youth, but all tends to make one believe in the vehemence of its passions. Beneath the Platonic calm of the sonnets there is latent a deep delight in carnal form and color. There, and still more in the madrigals, he often falls into the language of less tranquil affections; while some of them have the color of penitence, as from a wanderer returning home. He who spoke so decisively of the supremacy in the imaginative world of the unveiled human form had not been always a mere Platonic lover. Vague and wayward his loves may have been; but they partook of the strength of his nature, and sometimes would by no means become music, so that the comely order of his days was quite put out: *par che amaro ogni mio dolce io senta.*

But his genius is in harmony with itself; and just as in the products of his art we find resources of sweetness within their exceeding strength, so in his own story also, bitter as the ordinary sense of it may be, there are select pages shut in among the rest, pages one might easily turn over too lightly, but which yet sweeten the whole volume. The interest of Michelangelo's poems is that they make us spectators of this struggle; the struggle of a strong nature to adorn and attune itself; the struggle of a desolating passion, which yearns to be resigned and sweet and pensive, as Dante's was. It is a consequence of the occasional and informal character of his poetry, that it brings us nearer to himself, his own mind and temper, than any work done only to support a literary reputation could possibly do. His letters tell us little that is worth knowing about him, a few poor quarrels about money and commissions. But it is quite otherwise with these songs and sonnets, written down at odd moments, sometimes on the margins of his sketches, themselves often unfinished sketches, arresting some salient feeling, or unpremeditated idea, as it passed. And it happens that a true study of these has become within the last few years for the first time possible. A few of the sonnets circulated widely in manuscript, and became almost within Michelangelo's own lifetime a subject of academical discourses. But they were first collected in a volume in 1623, by the greatnephew of Michelangelo, Michelangelo Buonarroti the younger. He omitted much. rewrote the sonnets in part, and sometimes compressed vo or more compositions into one, always losing something of the force and incisiveness of the original. So the book remained, neglected even by Italians themselves in the last century, through the influence of that French taste which despised all compositions of the kind, as it despised and neglected Dante. *Sa réputation s'affirmera toujours*—Voltaire says of Dante—*parce qu'on ne le lit guère*. But in 1858, the last of the Buonarroti bequeathed to the municipality of Florence the curiosities of his family. Among them was a precious volume containing the autograph of the sonnets. A learned Italian, Signor Cesare Guasti, undertook to collate this autograph with other manuscripts at the Vatican and elsewhere, and in 1863 published a true version of Michelangelo's poems, with dissertations and a paraphrase.

People have often spoken of these poems as if they were a mere cry of distress, a lover's complaint over the obduracy of Vittoria Colonna. But those who speak thus forget that though it is quite possible that Michelangelo had seen Vittoria, that somewhat shadowy figure, as early as 1537, yet their closer intimacy did not begin till about the year 1542, when Michelangelo was nearly seventy years old. Vittoria herself, an ardent neo-Catholic, vowed to perpetual widowhood since the news had reached her, seventeen years before, that her husband, the youthful and princely Marquess of Pescara, lay dead of the wounds he had received in the battle of Pavia, was then no longer an object of great passion. In a dialogue written by the painter, Francesco d'Ollanda, we catch a glimpse of them together in an empty church at Rome, one Sunday afternoon, discussing indeed the characteristics of various schools of art, but still more the writings of Saint Paul, already following the ways, and tasting the sunless pleasures of weary people, whose hold on outward things is slackening. In a letter still extant he regrets that when he visited her after death he had kissed her hands only. He made, or set to work to make, a crucifix for her use, and two drawings, perhaps in preparation for it, are now in Oxford. From allusions in the sonnets, we may divine that when they first approached each other he had debated much with himself whether this last passion would be the most unsoftening, the most desolating of all—*un dolce amaro, un sì e no mi muovi;* is it carnal affection, or, *del suo prestino stato* (Plato's antenatal state) *il raggio ardente?* The older, conventional criticism, dealing with the text of 1623, had lightly assumed that all or nearly all the sonnets were actually addressed to Vittoria herself; but Signor Guasti finds only four, or at most five, which can be so attributed on genuine authority. Still, there are reasons which make him assign the majority of them to the period between 1542 and 1547, and we may regard the volume as a record of this resting place in Michelangelo's story. We know how Goethe escaped from the stress of sentiments too strong for him by making a book about them; and for Michelangelo, to write down his passionate thoughts at all, to make sonnets about them, was already in some measure to command, and have his way with them:

> *La vita del mia amor non è il cor mio,*
> *Ch'amor, di quel ch'io t'amo, è senza core.*

It was just because Vittoria raised no great passion that the space in his life where she reigns has such peculiar suavity; and the spirit of the sonnets is lost if we once take them out of that dreamy atmosphere in which men have things as they will, because the hold of all outward things upon them is faint and thin. Their prevailing tone is a calm and meditative sweetness. The cry of distress is indeed there, but as a mere residue, a trace of bracing chalybeate salt, just discernible in the song, which rises as a clear, sweet spring from a charmed space in his life.

This charmed and temperate space in Michelangelo's life, without which its excessive strength would have been so imperfect, which saves him from the judgment of Dante on those who *willfully lived in sadness,* is then a well-defined period there, reaching from the year 1542 to the year 1547, the year of Vittoria's death. In it, the lifelong effort to tranquillize his vehement emotions by withdrawing them into the region of ideal sentiment, becomes successful; and the significance of Vittoria in it is, that she realizes for him a type of affection which even in disappointment may charm and sweeten his spirit. In this effort to tranquillize and sweeten life by idealizing its vehement sentiments, there were two great traditional types, either of which an Italian of the sixteenth century might have followed. There was Dante, whose little book of the *Vita Nuova* had early become a pattern of imaginative love, maintained somewhat feebly by the later followers of Petrarch; and since Plato had become something more than a name in Italy, by the publication of the Latin translation of his works by Marsilio Ficino, there was the Platonic tradition also. Dante's belief in the resurrection of the body, through which, even in heaven, Beatrice loses for him no tinge of flesh color, or fold of raiment even, and the Platonic dream of the passage of the soul through one form of life after another, with its passionate haste to escape from the burden of bodily form altogether, are, for all effects of art or poetry, principles diametrically opposite. And it is the Platonic tradition rather than Dante's that has molded Michelangelo's verse. In many ways no sentiment could have been less like Dante's love for Beatrice than Michelangelo's for Vittoria Colonna. Dante's comes in early youth; Beatrice is a child, with the wistful, ambiguous vision of a child, with a character still unaccentuated by the influence of outward circumstances, almost expressionless. Vittoria is a woman already weary, in advanced age, of grave intellectual qualities. Dante's story is a piece of figured work, inlaid with lovely incidents. In Michelangelo's poems, frost and fire are almost the only images—the refining fire of the goldsmith; once or twice the phoenix; ice melting at the fire; fire struck from the rock which it afterwards consumes. Except one doubtful allusion to a journey, there are almost no incidents. But there is much of the bright, sharp, unerring skill, with which in boyhood he gave the look of age to the head of a faun by chipping a tooth from its jaw with a single stroke of the hammer. For Dante, the amiable and devout materialism of the Middle

Ages sanctifies all that is presented by hand and eye.
Michelangelo is always pressing forward from the outward
beauty *(il bel del fuor che agli occhi piace)* to apprehend
the unseen beauty *(trascenda nella forma universale)*—
that abstract form of beauty, about which the Platonists
reason. And this gives the impression in him of something
flitting and unfixed, of the houseless and complaining spirit,
almost clairvoyant through the frail and yielding flesh. He
accounts for love at first sight by a previous state of
existence—*la dove io t'amai prima.*

And yet there are many points in which he is really like
Dante, and comes very near to the original image, beyond
those later and feebler followers of Petrarch. He learns
from Dante rather than from Plato, that for lovers, the
surfeiting of desire *(ove gran desir gran copia affrena)* is
a state less happy than misery full of hope *(una miseria
di speranza piena).* He recalls him in the repetition of the
words *gentile* and *cortesia,* in the personification of *Amor,*
in the tendency to dwell minutely on the physical effects
of the presence of a beloved object on the pulses and the
heart. Above all, he resembles Dante in the warmth and
intensity of his political utterances, for the lady of one of
his noblest sonnets was from the first understood to be
the city of Florence; and he avers that all must be asleep
in heaven, if she, who was created *d'angelica forma,* for a
thousand lovers is appropriated by one alone, some Piero,
or Alessandro de' Medici. Once and again he introduces
Love and Death, who dispute concerning him; for, like
Dante and all the nobler souls of Italy, he is much occupied
with thoughts of the grave, and his true mistress is Death;
death at first as the worst of all sorrows and disgraces,
with a clod of the field for its brain; afterward, death in
its high distinction, its detachment from vulgar needs, the
angry stains of life and action escaping fast.

Some of those whom the gods love die young. This man,
because the gods loved him, lingered on to be of immense,
patriarchal age, till the sweetness it had taken so long to
secrete in him was found at last. Out of the strong came
forth sweetness—*ex forti dulcedo.* The world had changed
around him. The New Catholicism had taken the place of
the Renaissance. The spirit of the Roman church had
changed; in the vast world's cathedral which his skill had
helped to raise for it, it looked stronger than ever. Some

of the first members of the Oratory were among his intimate associates. They were of a spirit as unlike as possible from that of Lorenzo, or Savonarola even. The opposition of the Reformation to art has been often enlarged upon; far greater was that of the Catholic revival. But in thus fixing itself in a frozen orthodoxy, the Roman Catholic church had passed beyond him, and he was a stranger to it. In earlier days, when its beliefs had been in a fluid state, he too might have been drawn into the controversy; he might have been for spiritualizing the papal sovereignty, like Savonarola; or for adjusting the dreams of Plato and Homer with the words of Christ, like Pico della Mirandola. But things had moved onward, and such adjustments were no longer possible. For himself, he had long since fallen back on that divine ideal, which above the wear and tear of creeds has been forming itself for ages as the possession of nobler souls. And now he began to feel the soothing influence which since that time the Roman church has often exerted over spirits too noble to be its subjects, yet brought within the neighborhood of its action; consoled and tranquillized, as a traveler might be, resting for one evening in a strange city, by its stately aspect, and the sentiment of its many fortunes, just because with those fortunes he has nothing to do. So, he lingers on; a *revenant,* as the French say, a ghost out of another age, in a world too coarse to touch his faint sensibilities too closely; dreaming, in a worn-out society, theatrical in its life, theatrical in its art, theatrical even in its devotion, on the morning of the world's history, on the primitive form of man, on the images under which that primitive world had conceived of spiritual forces.

I have dwelt on the thought of Michelangelo as thus lingering beyond his time in a world not his own, because, if one is to distinguish the peculiar savor of his work, he must be approached, not through his followers, but through his predecessors; not through the marbles of Saint Peter's, but through the work of the sculptors of the fifteenth century over the tombs and altars of Tuscany. He is the last of the Florentines, of those on whom the peculiar sentiment of the Florence of Dante and Giotto descended; he is the consummate representative of the form that sentiment took in the fifteenth century with men like Luca

Signorelli, and Mino da Fiesole. Up to him the tradition of
sentiment is unbroken, the progress toward surer and more
mature methods of expressing that sentiment continuous.
But his professed disciples did not share this temper; they
are in love with his strength only, and seem not to feel
his grave and temperate sweetness. Theatricality is their
chief characteristic; and that is a quality as little attribut-
able to Michelangelo as to Mino, or Luca Signorelli. With
him, as with them, all is serious, passionate, impulsive.

This discipleship of Michelangelo, this dependence of
his on the tradition of the Florentine schools, is nowhere
seen more clearly than in his treatment of the Creation.
The *Creation of Man* had haunted the mind of the Middle
Ages like a dream; and weaving it into a hundred carved
ornaments of capital or doorway, the Italian sculptors had
early impressed upon it that pregnancy of expression
which seems to give it many veiled meanings. As with
other artistic conceptions of the Middle Ages, its treatment became almost conventional, handed on from artist
to artist, with slight changes, till it came to have almost an
independent, abstract existence of its own. It was characteristic of the medieval mind thus to give an independent
traditional existence to a special pictorial conception, or
to a legend, like that of Tristram or Tannhäuser, or even to
the very thoughts and substance of a book, like the *Imitation,* so that no single workman could claim it as his own,
and the book, the image, the legend, had itself a legend,
and its fortunes, and a personal history; and it is a sign of
the medievalism of Michelangelo, that he thus receives
from tradition his central conception, and does but add the
last touches, in transferring it to the frescoes of the Sistine
Chapel.

But there was another tradition of those earlier more
serious Florentines, of which Michelangelo is the inheritor,
to which he gives the final expression, and which centers
in the sacristy of San Lorenzo, as the tradition of the
Creation centers in the Sistine Chapel. It has been said
that all the great Florentines were preoccupied with death.
Outre-tombe! Outre-tombe! is the burden of their
thoughts, from Dante to Savanarola. Even the gay and
licentious Boccaccio gives a keener edge to his stories
by putting them in the mouths of a party of people who
had taken refuge from the plague in a country house. It

was to this inherited sentiment, this practical decision
that to be preoccupied with the thought of death was in
itself dignifying, and a note of high quality, that the
seriousness of the great Florentines of the fifteenth century
was partly due; and it was reinforced in them by the actual
sorrows of their times. How often, and in what various
ways, had they seen life stricken down, in their streets
and houses. *La bella Simonetta* dies in early youth, and
is borne to the grave with uncovered face. The young
Cardinal Jacopo di Portogallo dies on a visit to Florence
—*insignis formâ fui et mirabili modestiâ*—his epitaph
dares to say; Antonio Rossellino carves his tomb in the
church of San Miniato, with care for the shapely hands
and feet, and sacred attire; Luca della Robbia puts his
skyiest work there; and the tomb of the youthful and
princely prelate became the strangest and most beautiful
thing in that strange and beautiful place. After the execution of the Pazzi conspirators, Botticelli is employed to
paint their portraits. This preoccupation with serious
thoughts and sad images might easily have resulted, as it
did, for instance, in the gloomy villages of the Rhine, or
in the overcrowded parts of medieval Paris, as it still does
in many a village of the Alps, in something merely morbid
or grotesque, in the *Danse Macabre* of many French and
German painters, or the grim inventions of Dürer. From
such a result the Florentine masters of the fifteenth
century were saved by their high Italian dignity and
culture, and still more by their tender pity for the thing
itself. They must often have leaned over the lifeless body,
when all was at length quiet and smoothed out. After
death, it is said, the traces of slighter and more superficial
dispositions disappear; the lines become more simple and
dignified; only the abstract lines remain, in a great indifference. They came thus to see death in its distinction;
and following it perhaps one stage further, and dwelling
for a moment on the point where all that transitory dignity
broke up, and discerning with no clearness a new body,
they paused just in time, and abstained with a sentiment
of profound pity.

Of all this sentiment Michelangelo is the achievement;
and first of all, of pity. *Pietà*—pity—the pity of the Virgin
Mother over the dead body of Christ, expanded into the
pity of all mothers over all dead sons, the entombment,

with its cruel "hard stones," that is the subject of his predilection. He has left it in many forms, sketches, half-finished designs, finished and unfinished groups of sculpture; but always as a hopeless, rayless, almost heathen sorrow—no divine sorrow, but mere pity and awe at the stiff limbs and colorless lips. There is a drawing of his at Oxford, in which the dead body has sunk to the earth between his mother's feet, with the arms extended over her knees. The tombs in the sacristy of San Lorenzo are memorials, not of any of the nobler and greater Medici, but of Giuliano, and Lorenzo the younger, noticeable chiefly for their somewhat early death. It is mere human nature therefore which has prompted the sentiment here. The titles assigned traditionally to the four symbolical figures, *Night* and *Day, the Twilight* and *the Dawn*, are far too definite for them; they come much nearer to the mind and spirit of their author, and are a more direct expression of his thoughts, than any merely symbolical conceptions could possibly have been. They concentrate and express, less by way of definite conceptions than by the touches, the promptings of a piece of music, all those vague fancies, misgivings, presentiments, which shift and mix and define themselves and fade again, whenever the thoughts try to fix themselves with sincerity on the conditions and surroundings of the disembodied spirit. I suppose no one would come here for consolation; for seriousness, for solemnity, for dignity of impression perhaps, but not for consolation. It is a place neither of terrible nor consoling thoughts, but of vague and wistful speculation. Here again, Michelangelo is the disciple not so much of Dante as of the Platonists. Dante's belief in immortality is formal, precise, and firm, as much so almost as that of a child, who thinks the dead will hear if you cry loud enough. But in Michelangelo you have maturity, the mind of the grown man, dealing cautiously and dispassionately with serious things; and what hope he has is based on the consciousness of ignorance—ignorance of man, ignorance of the nature of the mind, its origin and capacities. Michelangelo is so ignorant of the spiritual world, of the new body and its laws, that he does not surely know whether the consecrated host may not be the body of Christ. And of all that range of sentiment he is the poet, a poet still alive, and in possession of our inmost thoughts—dumb inquiry over the relapse after death into the formlessness which preceded life, the change, the revolt from that change, then the correcting, hallowing, consoling rush of pity; at last, far off, thin and vague, yet not more vague than the most definite thoughts men have had through three centuries on a matter that has been so near their hearts, the new body—a passing light, a mere intangible, external effect, over those too rigid, or too formless faces; a dream that lingers a moment, retreating in the dawn, incomplete, aimless, helpless; a thing with faint hearing, faint memory, faint power of touch; a breath, a flame in the doorway, a feather in the wind.

The qualities of the great masters in art or literature, the combination of those qualities, the laws by which they moderate, support, relieve each other, are not peculiar to them; but most often typical standards, revealing instances of the laws by which certain aesthetic effects are produced. The old masters indeed are simpler; their characteristics are written larger, and are easier to read, than their analogues in all the mixed, confused productions of the modern mind. But when once we have succeeded in defining for ourselves those characteristics, and the law of their combination, we have acquired a standard or measure which helps us to put in its right place many a vagrant genius, many an unclassified talent, many precious though imperfect products of art. It is so with the components of the true character of Michelangelo. That strange interfusion of sweetness and strength is not to be found in those who claimed to be his followers; but it is found in many of those who worked before him, and in many others down to our own time, in William Blake, for instance, and Victor Hugo, who, though not of his school, and unaware, are his true sons, and help us to understand him, as he in turn interprets and justifies them. Perhaps this is the chief use in studying old masters.

LEONARDO DA VINCI

IN Vasari's life of Leonardo da Vinci as we now read it there are some variations from the first edition. There, the painter who has fixed the outward type of Christ for

succeeding centuries was a bold speculator, holding lightly
by other men's beliefs, setting philosophy above Christianity. Words of his, trenchant enough to justify this
impression, are not recorded, and would have been out
of keeping with a genius of which one characteristic is
the tendency to lose itself in a refined and graceful
mystery. The suspicion was but the time-honored form
in which the world stamps its appreciation of one who
has thoughts for himself alone, his high indifference, his
intolerance of the common form of things; and in the
second edition the image was changed into something
fainter and more conventional. But it is still by a certain
mystery in his work, and something enigmatical beyond
the usual measure of great men, that he fascinates, or
perhaps half repels. His life is one of sudden revolts,
with intervals in which he works not at all, or apart
from the main scope of his work. By a strange fortune
the works on which his more popular fame rested disappeared early from the world, as the *Battle of the Standard;*
or are mixed obscurely with the work of meaner hands,
as the *Last Supper.* His type of beauty is so exotic that
it fascinates a larger number than it delights, and seems
more than that of any other artist to reflect ideas and
views and some scheme of the world within; so that he
seemed to his contemporaries to be the possessor of
some unsanctified and secret wisdom; as, to Michelet
and others, to have anticipated modern ideas. He trifles
with his genius, and crowds all his chief work into a few
tormented years of later life; yet he is so possessed by
his genius that he passes unmoved through the most
tragic events, overwhelming his country and friends,
like one who comes across them by chance on some
secret errand.

His *legend,* as the French say, with the anecdotes
which everyone knows, is one of the most brilliant in
Vasari. Later writers merely copied it, until, in 1804,
Carlo Amoretti applied to it a criticism which left hardly
a date fixed, and not one of those anecdotes untouched.
The various questions thus raised have since that time
become, one after another, subjects of special study, and
mere antiquarianism has in this direction little more to
do. For others remain the editing of the thirteen books
of his manuscripts, and the separation by technical crit-

icism of what in his reputed works is really his, from what is only half his, or the work of his pupils. But a lover of strange souls may still analyze for himself the impression made on him by those works, and try to reach through it a definition of the chief elements of Leonardo's genius. The *legend,* corrected and enlarged by its critics, may now and then intervene to support the results of this analysis.

His life has three divisions—thirty years at Florence, nearly twenty years at Milan, then nineteen years of wandering, till he sinks to rest under the protection of Francis the First at the Château de Cloux. The dishonor of illegitimacy hangs over his birth. Piero Antonio, his father, was of a noble Florentine house, of Vinci in the Val d'Arno, and Leonardo, brought up delicately among the true children of that house, was the love child of his youth, with the keen, puissant nature such children often have. We see him in his youth fascinating all men by his beauty, improvising music and songs, buying the caged birds and setting them free, as he walked the streets of Florence, fond of odd bright dresses and spirited horses.

From his earliest years he designed many objects, and constructed models in relief, of which Vasari mentions some of women smiling. His father, pondering over this promise in the child, took him to the workshop of Andrea del Verrocchio, then the most famous artist in Florence. Beautiful objects lay about there—reliquaries, pyxes, silver images for the pope's chapel at Rome, strange fancywork of the Middle Ages, keeping odd company with fragments of antiquity, then but lately discovered. Another student Leonardo may have seen there—a boy into whose soul the level light and aerial illusions of Italian sunsets had passed, in after days famous as Perugino. Verrocchio was an artist of the earlier Florentine type, carver, painter, and worker in metals, in one; designer, not of pictures only, but of all things for sacred or household use, drinking vessels, ambries, instruments of music, making them all fair to look upon, filling the common ways of life with the reflection of some faroff brightness; and years of patience had refined his hand till his work was now sought after from distant places. It happened that Verrocchio was employed by the brethren of Vallombrosa to paint the Baptism of Christ, and Leonardo was allowed to finish an angel in the left-hand corner. It was one of those moments in which the progress of a great thing—here, that of the art of Italy —presses hard and sharp on the happiness of an individual, through whose discouragement and decrease, humanity, in more fortunate persons, comes a step nearer to its final success.

For beneath the cheerful exterior of the mere well-paid craftsman, chasing brooches for the copes of Santa Maria Novella, or twisting metal screens for the tombs of the Medici, lay the ambitious desire of expanding the destiny of Italian art by a larger knowledge and insight into things, a purpose in art not unlike Leonardo's still unconscious purpose; and often, in the modeling of drapery, or of a lifted arm, or of hair cast back from the face, there came to him something of the freer manner and richer humanity of a later age. But in this *Baptism* the pupil had surpassed the master; and Verrocchio turned away as one stunned, and as if his sweet earlier work must thereafter be distasteful to him, from the bright animated angel of Leonardo's hand.

The angel may still be seen in Florence, a space of sunlight in the cold, labored old picture; but the legend is true only in sentiment, for painting had always been the art by which Verrocchio set least store. And as in a sense he anticipates Leonardo, so to the last Leonardo recalls the studio of Verrocchio, in the love of beautiful toys, such as the vessel of water for a mirror, and lovely needlework about the implicated hands in the *Modesty and Vanity,* and of reliefs, like those cameos which in the *Virgin of the Balances* hang all round the girdle of Saint Michael, and of bright variegated stones, such as the agates in the *Saint Anne,* and in a hieratic preciseness and grace, as of a sanctuary swept and garnished. Amid all the cunning and intricacy of his Lombard manner this never left him. Much of it there must have been in that lost picture of *Paradise,* which he prepared as a cartoon for tapestry, to be woven in the looms of Flanders. It was the perfection of the older Florentine style of miniature painting, with patient putting of each leaf upon the trees and each flower in the grass, where the first man and woman were standing.

And because it was the perfection of that style, it awoke in Leonardo some seed of discontent which lay in the secret places of his nature. For the way to perfection is through a series of disgusts; and this picture—all that he had done so far in his life at Florence—was after all in the old slight manner. His art, if it was to be something in the world, must be weighted with more of the meaning of nature and purpose of humanity. Nature was "the true mistress of higher intelligences." So he plunged into the study of nature. And in doing this he followed the manner of the older students; he brooded over the hidden virtues of plants and crystals, the lines traced by the stars as they moved in the sky, over the correspondences which exist between the different orders of living things, through which, to eyes opened, they interpret each other; and for years he seemed to those about him as one listening to a voice, silent for other men.

He learned here the art of going deep, of tracking the sources of expression to their subtlest retreats, the power of an intimate presence in the things he handled. He did not at once or entirely desert his art; only he was no longer the cheerful, objective painter, through whose soul, as through clear glass, the bright figures of Florentine life, only made a little mellower and more pensive by the transit, passed onto the white wall. He wasted many days in curious tricks of design, seeming to lose himself in the spinning of intricate devices of lines and colors. He was smitten with a love of the impossible—the perforation of mountains, changing the course of rivers, raising great buildings, such as the church of San Giovanni, in the air; all those feats for the performance of which natural magic professes to have the key. Later writers, indeed, see in these efforts an anticipation of modern mechanics; in him they were rather dreams, thrown off by the overwrought and laboring brain. Two ideas were especially fixed in him, as reflexes of things that had touched his brain in childhood beyond the measure of other impressions—the smiling of women and the motion of great waters.

And in such studies some interfusion of the extremes of beauty and terror shaped itself, as an image that might be seen and touched, in the mind of this gracious youth, so fixed that for the rest of his life it never left him;

and as catching glimpses of it in the strange eyes or hair of chance people, he would follow such about the streets of Florence till the sun went down, of whom many sketches of his remain. Some of these are full of a curious beauty, that remote beauty apprehended only by those who have sought it carefully; who, starting with acknowledged types of beauty, have refined as far upon these, as these refine upon the world of common forms. But mingled inextricably with this there is an element of mockery also; so that, whether in sorrow or scorn, he caricatures Dante even. Legions of grotesques sweep under his hand; for has not nature too her grotesques— the rent rock, the distorting light of evening on lonely roads, the unveiled structure of man in the embryo, or the skeleton?

All these swarming fancies unite in the *Medusa* of the Uffizi. Vasari's story of an earlier Medusa, painted on a wooden shield, is perhaps an invention; and yet, properly told, has more of the air of truth about it than anything else in the whole legend. For its real subject is not the serious work of a man, but the experiment of a child. The lizards and glowworms and other strange small creatures which haunt an Italian vineyard bring before one the whole picture of a child's life in a Tuscan dwelling, half castle, half farm; and are as true to nature as the pretended astonishment of the father for whom the boy has prepared a surprise. It was not in play that he painted that other Medusa, the one great picture which he left behind him in Florence. The subject has been treated in various ways; Leonardo alone cuts to its center; he alone realizes it as the head of a corpse, exercising its powers through all the circumstances of death. What may be called the fascination of corruption penetrates in every touch its exquisitely finished beauty. About the dainty lines of the cheek the bat flits unheeded. The delicate snakes seem literally strangling each other in terrified struggle to escape from the Medusa brain. The hue which violent death always brings with it is in the features: features singularly massive and grand, as we catch them inverted, in a dexterous foreshortening, sloping upward, almost sliding down upon us, crown foremost, like a great calm stone against which the wave of serpents breaks. But it is a subject that may well be left to the beautiful verses of Shelley.

The science of that age was all divination, clairvoyance, unsubjected to our exact modern formulas, seeking in an instant of vision to concentrate a thousand experiences. Later writers, thinking only of the well-ordered treatise on painting which a Frenchman, Raffaelle du Fresne, a hundred years afterwards, compiled from Leonardo's bewildered manuscripts, written strangely, as his manner was, from right to left, have imagined a rigid order in his inquiries. But this rigid order was little in accordance with the restlessness of his character; and if we think of him as the mere reasoner who subjects design to anatomy, and composition to mathematical rules, we shall hardly have of him that impression which those about him received from him. Poring over his crucibles, making experiments with color, trying by a strange variation of the alchemist's dream to discover the secret, not of an elixir to make man's natural life immortal, but rather of giving immortality to the subtlest and most delicate effects of painting, he seemed to them rather the sorcerer or the magician, possessed of curious secrets and a hidden knowledge, living in a world of which he alone possessed the key. What his philosophy seems to have been most like is that of Paracelsus or Cardan; and much of the spirit of the older alchemy still hangs about it, with its confidence in short cuts and odd byways to knowledge. To him philosophy was to be something giving strange swiftness and double sight, divining the sources of springs beneath the earth or of expression beneath the human countenance, clairvoyant of occult gifts in common or uncommon things, in the reed at the brookside, or the star which draws near to us but once in a century. How, in this way, the clear purpose was overclouded, the fine chaser's hand perplexed, we but dimly see; the mystery which at no point quite lifts from Leonardo's life is deepest here. But it is certain that at one period of his life he had almost ceased to be an artist.

The year 1483—the year of the birth of Raphael and the thirty-first of Leonardo's life—is fixed as the date of his visit to Milan by the letter in which he recommends himself to Lodovico Sforza, and offers to tell him, for a price, strange secrets in the art of war. It was that Sforza who murdered his young nephew by slow poison, yet was so susceptible of religious impressions that he blended mere earthly passions with a sort of religious sentimentalism, and who took for his device the mulberry tree—symbol, in its long delay and sudden yielding of flowers and fruit together, of a wisdom which economizes all forces for an opportunity of sudden and sure effect. The fame of Leonardo had gone before him, and he was to model a colossal statue of Francesco, the first duke of Milan. As for Leonardo himself, he came not as an artist at all, or careful of the fame of one; but as a player on the harp, a strange harp of silver of his own construction, shaped in some curious likeness to a horse's skull. The capricious spirit of Lodovico was susceptible also of the charm of music, and Leonardo's nature had a kind of spell in it. Fascination is always the word descriptive of him. No portrait of his youth remains; but all tends to make us believe that up to this time some charm of voice and aspect, strong enough to balance the disadvantage of his birth, had played about him. His physical strength was great; it was said that he could bend a horseshoe like a coil of lead.

The Duomo, the work of artists from beyond the Alps, so fantastic to the eye of a Florentine, used to the mellow, unbroken surfaces of Giotto and Arnolfo, was then in all its freshness; and below, in the streets of Milan, moved a people as fantastic, changeful, and dreamlike. To Leonardo least of all men could there be anything poisonous in the exotic flowers of sentiment which grew there. It was a life of brilliant sins and exquisite amusements—Leonardo became a celebrated designer of pageants—and it suited the quality of his genius, composed in almost equal parts of curiosity and the desire of beauty, to take things as they came.

Curiosity and the desire of beauty—these are the two elementary forces in Leonardo's genius; curiosity often in conflict with the desire of beauty, but generating, in union with it, a type of subtle and curious grace.

The movement of the fifteenth century was twofold; partly the Renaissance, partly also the coming of what is called the "modern spirit," with its realism, its appeal to experience, it comprehended a return to antiquity,

and a return to nature. Raphael represents the return to
antiquity, and Leonardo the return to nature. In this
return to nature, he was seeking to satisfy a boundless
curiosity by her perpetual surprises, a microscopic sense
of finish by her finesse, or delicacy of operation, that
subtilitas naturae which Bacon notices. So we find him
often in intimate relations with men of science, with Fra
Luca Paccioli the mathematician, and the anatomist Marc
Antonio della Torre. His observations and experiments
fill thirteen volumes of manuscript; and those who can
judge describe him as anticipating long before, by rapid
intuition, the later ideas of science. He explained the
obscure light of the unilluminated part of the moon, knew
that the sea had once covered the mountains which contain shells, and the gathering of the equatorial waters
above the polar.

He who thus penetrated into the most secret parts of
nature preferred always the more to the less remote,
what, seeming exceptional, was an instance of law more
refined, the construction about things of a peculiar atmosphere and mixed lights. He paints flowers with such
curious felicity that different writers have attributed to
him a fondness for particular flowers, as Clement the
cyclamen, and Rio the jasmine; while, at Venice, there
is a stray leaf from his portfolio dotted all over with
studies of violets and the wild rose. In him first, appears
the taste for what is bizarre or *recherché* in landscape;
hollow places full of the green shadow of bituminous
rocks, ridged reefs of trap-rock which cut the water into
quaint sheets of light—their exact antitype is in our own
western seas; all the solemn effects of moving water; you
may follow it springing from its distant source among the
rocks on the heath of the *Madonna of the Balances,*
passing as a little fall into the treacherous calm of the
Madonna of the Lake, next, as a goodly river, below the
cliffs of the *Madonna of the Rocks,* washing the white
walls of its distant villages, stealing out in a network of
divided streams in *La Gioconda* to the seashore of the
Saint Anne—that delicate place, where the wind passes
like the hand of some fine etcher over the surface, and
the untorn shells are lying thick upon the sand, and the
tops of the rocks, to which the waves never rise, are
green with grass, grown as fine as hair. It is the landscape,

not of dreams or of fancy, but of places far withdrawn, and hours selected from a thousand with a miracle of finesse. Through Leonardo's strange veil of sight things reach him so; in no ordinary night or day, but as in faint light of eclipse, or in some brief interval of falling rain at daybreak, or through deep water.

And not into nature only; but he plunged also into human personality, and became above all a painter of portraits; faces of a modeling more skillful than has been seen before or since, embodied with a reality which almost amounts to illusion, on dark air. To take a character as it was, and delicately sound its stops, suited one so curious in observation, curious in invention. So he painted the portraits of Lodovico's mistresses, Lucretia Crivelli and Cecilia Galerani the poetess, of Lodovico himself, and the Duchess Beatrice. The portrait of Cecilia Galerani is lost, but that of Lucretia Crivelli has been identified with *La Belle Feronière* of the Louvre, and Lodovico's pale, anxious face still remains in the Ambrosian Library. Opposite is the portrait of Beatrice d'Este, in whom Leonardo seems to have caught some presentiment of early death, painting her precise and grave, full of the refinement of the dead, in sad earth-colored raiment, set with pale stones.

Sometimes this curiosity came in conflict with the desire of beauty; it tended to make him go too far below that outside of things in which art begins and ends. This struggle between the reason and its ideas, and the senses, the desire of beauty, is the key to Leonardo's life at Milan —his restlessness, his endless retouchings, his odd experiments with color. How much must he leave unfinished, how much recommence! His problem was the transmutation of ideas into images. What he had attained so far had been the mastery of that earlier Florentine style, with its naive and limited sensuousness. Now he was to entertain in this narrow medium those divinations of a humanity too wide for it, that larger vision of the opening world, which is only not too much for the great, irregular art of Shakespeare; and everywhere the effort is visible in the work of his hands. This agitation, this perpetual delay, give him an air of weariness and ennui. To others he seems to be aiming at an impossible effect, to do something that art, that painting, can never do.

Often the expression of physical beauty at this or that point seems strained and marred in the effort, as in those heavy German foreheads—too heavy and German for perfect beauty.

For there was a touch of Germany in that genius which, as Goethe said, had *müde sich gedacht* ("thought itself weary"). What an anticipation of modern Germany, for instance, in that debate on the question whether sculpture or painting is the nobler art.* But there is this difference between him and the German, that, with all that curious science, the German would have thought nothing more was needed; and the name of Goethe himself reminds one how great for the artist may be the danger of overmuch science; how Goethe, who, in the *Elective Affinities* and the first part of *Faust,* does transmute ideas into images, who wrought many such transmutations, did not invariably find the spell-word, and in the second part of *Faust* presents us with a mass of science which has almost no artistic characters at all. But Leonardo will never work till the happy moment comes—that moment of *bien-être,* which to imaginative men is a moment of invention. On this moment he waits; other moments are but a preparation, or aftertaste of it. Few men distinguish between them as jealously as he did. Hence, so many flaws even in the choicest work. But for Leonardo the distinction is absolute, and, in the moment of *bien-être,* the alchemy complete; the idea is stricken into color and imagery; a cloudy mysticism is refined to a subdued and graceful mystery, and painting pleases the eye while it satisfies the soul.

This curious beauty is seen above all in his drawings, and in these chiefly in the abstract grace of the bounding lines. Let us take some of these drawings, and pause over them awhile; and, first, one of those at Florence—the heads of a woman and a little child, set side by side, but each in its own separate frame. First of all, there is much pathos in the reappearance in the fuller curves of the face of the child, of the sharper, more chastened lines of the worn and older face, which leaves no doubt that the heads are those of a little child and its mother. A feeling

* How princely, how characteristic of Leonardo, the answer: *Quanto più, un' arte porta seco fatica di corpo, tanto più è vile!*

for maternity is indeed always characteristic of Leonardo; and this feeling is further indicated here by the half-humorous pathos of the diminutive, rounded shoulders of the child. You may note a like pathetic power in drawings of a young man, seated in a stooping posture, his face in his hands, as in sorrow; of a slave sitting in an uneasy inclined posture, in some brief interval of rest; of a small Madonna and Child, peeping sideways in half-reassured terror, as a mighty griffin with batlike wings, one of Leonardo's finest *inventions,* descends suddenly from the air to snatch up a lion wandering near them. But note in these, as that which especially belongs to art, the contour of the young man's hair, the poise of the slave's arm above his head, and the curves of the head of the child, following the little skull within, thin and fine as some seashell worn by the wind.

Take again another head, still more full of sentiment, but of a different kind, a little drawing in red chalk which everyone remembers who has examined at all carefully the drawings by old masters at the Louvre. It is a face of doubtful sex, set in the shadow of its own hair, the cheekline in high light against it, with something voluptuous and full in the eyelids and the lips. Another drawing might pass for the same face in childhood, with parched and feverish lips, but with much sweetness in the loose, short-waisted childish dress, with necklace and *bulla,* and in the daintily bound hair. We might take the thread of suggestion which these two drawings offer, when thus set side by side, following it through the drawings at Florence, Venice, and Milan, construct a sort of series, illustrating better than anything else Leonardo's type of womanly beauty. Daughters of Herodias, with their fantastic headdresses knotted and folded so strangely, to leave the dainty oval of the face disengaged, they are not of the Christian family, or of Raphael's. They are the clairvoyants, through whom, as through delicate instruments, one becomes aware of the subtler forces of nature, and the modes of their action, all that is magnetic in it, all those finer conditions wherein material things rise to that subtlety of operation which constitutes them spiritual, where only the finer nerve and the keener touch can follow; it is as if in certain revealing instances we actually saw them at their work on human flesh. Nervous, electric, faint always with some inexplicable faintness, they seem to be subject to exceptional conditions, to feel powers at work in the common air unfelt by others, to become, as it were, receptables of them, and pass them on to us in a chain of secret influences.

But among the more youthful heads there is one at Florence, which Love chooses for its own—the head of a young man, which may well be the likeness of Andrea Salaino, beloved of Leonardo for his curled and waving hair—*belli capelli ricci e inanellati*—and afterward his favorite pupil and servant. Of all the interests in living men and women which may have filled his life at Milan, this attachment alone is recorded; and in return, Salaino identified himself so entirely with Leonardo, that the picture of *Saint Anne,* in the Louvre, has been attributed to him. It illustrates Leonardo's usual choice of pupils, men of some natural charm of person or intercourse like Salaino, or men of birth, and princely habits of life like Francesco Melzi—men with just enough genius to be capable of initiation into his secret, for the sake of which they were ready to efface their own individuality. Among them, retiring often to the villa of the Melzi at Canonica al Vaprio, he worked at his fugitive manuscripts and sketches, working for the present hour, and for a few only, perhaps chiefly for himself. Other artists have been as careless of present or future applause, in self-forgetfulness, or because they set moral or political ends above the ends of art; but in him this solitary culture of beauty seems to have hung upon a kind of self-love, and a carelessness in the work of art of all but art itself. Out of the secret places of a unique temperament he brought strange blossoms and fruits hitherto unknown; and for him, the novel impression conveyed, the exquisite effect woven, counted as an end in itself—a perfect end.

And these pupils of his acquired his manner so thoroughly, that though the number of Leonardo's authentic works is very small indeed, there is a multitude of other men's pictures, through which we undoubtedly see him, and come very near to his genius. Sometimes, as in the little picture of the *Madonna of the Balances,* in which, from the bosom of his mother, Christ is weighing the pebbles of the brook against the sins of men, we have a hand, rough enough by contrast, working upon some

fine hint or sketch of his. Sometimes, as in the subjects of
the *Daughter of Herodias* and the *Head of John the
Baptist,* the lost originals have been re-echoed and varied
upon again and again by Luini and others. At other times
the original remains, but has been a mere theme or
motive, a type of which the accessories might be modified
or changed; and these variations have but brought out
the more the purpose, or expression of the original. It is
so with the so-called *Saint John the Baptist* of the Louvre
—one of the few naked figures Leonardo painted—whose
delicate brown flesh and woman's hair no one would go
out into the wilderness to seek, and whose treacherous
smile would have us understand something far beyond
the outward gesture, or circumstance. But the long, reedlike cross in the hand, which suggests Saint John the
Baptist, becomes faint in a copy at the Ambrosian Library, and disappears altogether in another, in the Palazzo
Rosso at Genoa. Returning from the last to the original,
we are no longer surprised by Saint John's strange likeness to the *Bacchus* which hangs near it, which set Théo-
phile Gautier thinking of Heine's notion of decayed gods,
who, to maintain themselves, after the fall of paganism,
took employment in the new religion. We recognize one
of those symbolical inventions in which the ostensible subject is used, not as matter for definite pictorial realization,
but as the starting point of a train of sentiment, as subtle
and vague as a piece of music. No one ever ruled over
his subject more entirely than Leonardo, or bent it more
dexterously to purely artistic ends. And so it comes to
pass that though he handles sacred subjects continually,
he is the most profane of painters; the given person or
subject, Saint John in the Desert, or the Virgin on the
knees of Saint Anne, is often merely the pretext for a
kind of work which carries one quite out of the range
of its conventional associations.

About the *Last Supper,* its decay and restorations, a whole
literature has risen up, Goethe's pensive sketch of its sad
fortunes being far the best. The death in childbirth of
the Duchess Beatrice was followed in Lodovico by one
of those paroxysms of religious feeling which in him were
constitutional. The low, gloomy Dominican church of
Saint Mary of the Graces had been the favorite shrine
of Beatrice. She had spent her last days there, full of

sinister presentiments; at last it had been almost necessary
to remove her from it by force; and now it was here that
mass was said a hundred times a day for her repose. On
the damp wall of the refectory, oozing with mineral salts,
Leonardo painted the *Last Supper*. A hundred anecdotes
were told about it, his retouchings and delays. They show
him refusing to work except at the moment of invention,
scornful of whoever thought that art was a work of mere
industry and rule, often coming the whole length of Milan
to give a single touch. He painted it, not in fresco, where
all must be impromptu, but in oils, the new method which
he had been one of the first to welcome, because it allowed of so many afterthoughts, so refined a working out
of perfection. It turned out that on a plastered wall no
process could have been less durable. Within fifty years
it had fallen into decay. And now we have to turn back
to Leonardo's own studies, above all, to one drawing of
the central head at the Brera, which in a union of tenderness and severity in the face lines, reminds one of the
monumental work of Mino da Fiesole, to trace it as it was.

It was another effort to set a given subject out of the
range of its conventional associations. Strange, after all
the misrepresentations of the Middle Ages, was the effort
to see it, not as the pale host of the altar, but as one
taking leave of his friends. Five years afterwards, the
young Raphael, at Florence, painted it with sweet and
solemn effect in the refectory of Saint Onofrio; but still
with all the mystical unreality of the school of Perugino.
Vasari pretends that the central head was never finished;
but finished or unfinished, or owing part of its effect to a
mellowing decay, this central head does but consummate
the sentiment of the whole company; ghosts through
which you see the wall, faint as the shadows of the leaves
upon the wall on autumn afternoons—this figure is but
the faintest, most spectral of them all. It is the image of
what the history it symbolizes has been more and more
ever since, paler and paler as it recedes from us. Criticism
came with its appeal from mystical unrealities to originals,
and restored no lifelike reality but these transparent
shadows, spirits which have not flesh and bones.

The *Last Supper* was finished in 1497; in 1498 the
French entered Milan, and whether or not the Gascon
bowmen used it as a mark for their arrows, the model

of Francesco Sforza certainly did not survive. What, in that age, such work was capable of being, of what nobility, amid what racy truthfulness to fact, we may judge from the bronze statue of Bartolomeo Colleoni on horseback, modeled by Leonardo's master, Verrocchio—he died of grief, it was said, because, the mold accidentally failing, he was unable himself to complete it—still standing in the piazza of Saint John and Saint Paul at Venice. Some traces of the thing may remain in certain of Leonardo's drawings, and also, perhaps, by a singular circumstance, in a faroff town of France. For Lodovico became a prisoner, and ended his days at Loches in Touraine; allowed, it is said, at last to breathe fresher air for awhile in one of the rooms of a high tower there, after many years of captivity in the dungeons below, where all seems sick with barbarous feudal memories, and where his prison is still shown, its walls covered with strange painted arabesques, ascribed by tradition to his hand, amused a little thus through the tedious years—vast helmets and faces and pieces of armor, among which in great letters the motto *Infelix Sum*, is woven in and out, and in which perhaps it is not too fanciful to see the fruit of a wistful afterdreaming over all those experiments with Leonardo on the armed figure of the great duke, which had occupied the two so often, during the days of his fortune at Milan.

The remaining years of Leonardo's life are more or less years of wandering. From his brilliant life at court he had saved nothing, and he returned to Florence a poor man. Perhaps necessity kept his spirit excited: the next four years are one prolonged rapture or ecstasy of invention. He painted the pictures of the Louvre, his most authentic works, which came there straight from the cabinet of Francis the First, at Fontainebleau. One picture of his, the *Saint Anne*—not the *Saint Anne* of the Louvre, but a mere cartoon, now in London—revived for a moment a sort of appreciation more common in an earlier time, when good pictures had still seemed miraculous; and for two days a crowd of people of all qualities passed in naive excitement through the chamber where it hung, and gave Leonardo a taste of Cimabue's triumph. But his work was less with the saints than with the living women of Florence; for he lived still in the polished society that he loved, and in the houses of Florence, left perhaps a little subject to light thoughts by the death of Savonarola, (the latest gossip is of an undraped Mona Lisa, found in some out-of-the-way corner of the late Orléans collection) he saw Ginevra di Benci, and Lisa, the young third wife of Francesco del Giocondo. As we have seen him using incidents of the sacred legend, not for their own sake, or as mere subjects for pictorial realization, but as a symbolical language for fancies all his own, so now he found a vent for his thoughts in taking one of these languid women, and raising her, as Leda or Pomona, Modesty or Vanity, to the seventh heaven of symbolical expression.

La Gioconda is, in the truest sense, Leonardo's masterpiece, the revealing instance of his mode of thought and work. In suggestiveness, only the *Melancholia* of Dürer is comparable to it; and no crude symbolism disturbs the effect of its subdued and graceful mystery. We all know the face and hands of the figure, set in its marble chair, in that cirque of fantastic rocks, as in some faint light under sea. Perhaps of all ancient pictures time has chilled it least.* As often happens with works in which invention seems to reach its limit, there is an element in it given to, not invented by, the master. In that inestimable folio of drawings, once in the possession of Vasari, were certain designs by Verrocchio, faces of such impressive beauty that Leonardo in his boyhood copied them many times. It is hard not to connect with these designs of the elder, by-passed master, as with its germinal principle, the unfathomable smile, always with a touch of something sinister in it, which plays over all Leonardo's work. Besides, the picture is a portrait. From childhood we see this image defining itself on the fabric of his dreams; and but for express historical testimony, we might fancy that this was but his ideal lady, embodied and beheld at last. What was the relationship of a living Florentine to this creature of his thought? By means of what strange affinities had the person and the dream grown up thus apart, and yet so closely together? Present from the first, incorporeal in Leonardo's thought, dimly traced in the designs of Verrocchio, she is found present at last in Il

* Yet for Vasari there was some further magic of crimson in the lips and cheeks, lost for us.

Giocondo's house. That there is much of mere portraiture in the picture is attested by the legend that by artificial means, the presence of mimes and flute players, that subtle expression was protracted on the face. Again, was it in four years, and by renewed labor never really completed, or in four months, and as by stroke of magic, that the image was projected?

The presence that thus rose so strangely beside the waters, is expressive of what in the ways of a thousand years man had come to desire. Hers is the head upon which all "the ends of the world are come," and the eyelids are a little weary. It is a beauty wrought out from within upon the flesh, the deposit, little cell by cell, of strange thoughts and fantastic reveries and exquisite passions. Set it for a moment beside one of those white Greek goddesses or beautiful women of antiquity, and how would they be troubled by this beauty, into which the soul with all its maladies has passed? All the thoughts and experience of the world have etched and molded there, in that which they have of power to refine and make expressive the outward form, the animalism of Greece, the lust of Rome, the reverie of the Middle Ages with its spiritual ambition and imaginative loves, the return of the pagan world, the sins of the Borgias. She is older than the rocks among which she sits; like the vampire, she has been dead many times, and learned the secrets of the grave; and has been a diver in deep seas, and keeps their fallen day about her; and trafficked for strange webs with Eastern merchants; and, as Leda, was the mother of Helen of Troy, and, as Saint Anne, the mother of Mary; and all this has been to her but as the sound of lyres and flutes, and lives only in the delicacy with which it has molded the changing lineaments, and tinged the eyelids and the hands. The fancy of a perpetual life, sweeping together ten thousand experiences, is an old one; and modern thought has conceived the idea of humanity as wrought upon by, and summing up in itself, all modes of thought and life. Certainly Lady Lisa might stand as the embodiment of the old fancy, the symbol of the modern idea.

During these years at Florence, Leonardo's history is the history of his art; he himself is lost in the bright cloud of it. The outward history begins again in 1502, with a wild journey through central Italy, which he makes as the chief engineer of Cesare Borgia. The biographer, putting together the stray jottings of his manuscripts, may follow him through every day of it, up the strange tower of Siena, which looks toward Rome, elastic like a bent bow, down to the seashore at Piombino, each place appearing as fitfully as in a fever dream.

One other great work was left for him to do, a work all trace of which soon vanished, *The Battle of the Standard,* in which he had Michelangelo for his rival. The citizens of Florence, desiring to decorate the walls of the great council chamber, had offered the work for competition, and any subject might be chosen from the Florentine wars of the fifteenth century. Michelangelo chose for his cartoon an incident of the war with Pisa, in which the Florentine soldiers, bathing in the Arno, are surprised by the sound of trumpets, and run to arms. His design has reached us only in an old engraving, which perhaps helps us less than what we remember of the background of his *Holy Family* in the Uffizi to imagine in what superhuman form, such as might have beguiled the heart of an earlier world, those figures may have risen from the water. Leonardo chose an incident from the battle of Anghiari, in which two parties of soldiers fight for a standard. Like Michelangelo's, his cartoon is lost, and has come to us only in sketches, and in a fragment of Rubens. Through the accounts given we may discern some lust of terrible things in it, so that even the horses tore each other with their teeth; and yet one fragment of it, in a drawing of his at Florence, is far different—a waving field of lovely armor, the chased edgings running like lines of sunlight from side to side. Michelangelo was twenty-seven years old; Leonardo more than fifty; and Raphael, then nineteen years old, visiting Florence for the first time, came and watched them as they worked.

We catch a glimpse of him again, at Rome in 1514, surrounded by his mirrors and vials and furnaces, making strange toys that seemed alive of wax and quicksilver. The hesitation which had haunted him all through life, and made him like one under a spell, was upon him now with double force. No one had ever carried political indifferentism farther; it had always been his philosophy to "fly before the storm"; he is for the Sforzas, or against them, as the tide of their fortune turns. Yet now in the political society of Rome, he came to be suspected of concealed French sympathies. It paralyzed him to find himself among enemies; and he turned wholly to France, which had long courted him.

France was about to become an Italy more Italian than Italy itself. Francis the First, like Lewis the Twelfth before him, was attracted by the finesse of Leonardo's work; *La Gioconda* was already in his cabinet, and he offered Leonardo the little Château de Cloux, with its vineyards and meadows, in the pleasant valley of the Masse, just outside the walls of the town of Amboise, where, especially in the hunting season, the court then frequently resided. *A Monsieur Lyonard, peinteur du Roy pour Amboyse*—so the letter of Francis the First is headed. It opens a prospect, one of the most attractive in the history of art, where, under a strange mixture of lights, Italian art dies away as a French exotic.

Two questions remain, after much busy antiquarianism, concerning Leonardo's death—the question of the form of his religion, and the question whether Francis the First was present at the time. They are of about equally little importance in the estimate of Leonardo's genius. The directions in his will about the thirty masses and the great candles for the church of Saint Florentin are things of course, their real purpose being immediate and practical; and on no theory of religion could these hurried offices be of much consequence. We forget them in speculating how one who had been always so desirous of beauty, but desired it always in such definite and precise forms, as hands or flowers or hair, looked forward now into the vague land, and experienced the last curiosity.

THE SCHOOL OF GIORGIONE

IT is the mistake of much popular criticism to regard poetry, music, and painting—all the various products of art—as but translations into different languages of one and the same fixed quantity of imaginative thought, supplemented by certain technical qualities of color, in painting; of sound, in music; of rhythmical words, in poetry. In this way, the sensuous element in art, and with it almost everything in art that is essentially artistic, is made a matter of indifference; and a clear apprehension of the opposite principle—that the sensuous material of each art brings with it a special phase or quality of beauty, untranslatable into the forms of any other, an order of impressions distinct in kind—is the beginning of all true aesthetic criticism. For, as art addresses not pure sense, still less the pure intellect, but the "imaginative reason" through the senses, there are differences of kind in aesthetic beauty, corresponding to the differences in kind of the gifts of sense themselves. Each art, therefore, having its own peculiar and untranslatable sensuous charm, has its own special mode of reaching the imagination, its own special responsibilities to its material. One of the functions of aesthetic criticism is to define these limitations; to estimate the degree in which a given work of art fulfills its responsibilities to its special material; to note in a picture that true pictorial charm, which is neither a mere poetical thought or sentiment, on the one hand, nor a mere result of communicable technical skill in color or design, on the other; to define in a poem that true poetical quality, which is neither descriptive nor meditative merely, but comes of an inventive handling of rhythmical language, the element of song in the singing; to note in music the musical charm, that essential music, which presents no words, no matter of sentiment or thought, separable from the special form in which it is conveyed to us.

To such a philosophy of the variations of the beautiful, Lessing's analysis of the spheres of sculpture and poetry, in the *Laokoon,* was an important contribution. But a true appreciation of these things is possible only in the light of a whole system of such art casuistries. Now painting is the art in the criticism of which this truth most needs enforcing, for it is in popular judgments on pictures that the false generalization of all art into forms of poetry is most prevalent. To suppose that all is mere technical acquirement in delineation or touch, working through and addressing itself to the intelligence, on the one side, or a merely poetical, or what may be called literary interest, addressed also to the pure intelligence, on the other: this is the way of most spectators, and of many critics, who have never caught sight all the time of that true pictorial quality which

lies between, unique pledge, as it is, of the possession of
the pictorial gift, that inventive or creative handling of
pure line and color, which, as almost always in Dutch
painting, as often also in the works of Titian or Veronese,
is quite independent of anything definitely poetical in the
subject it accompanies. It is the *drawing*—the design projected from the peculiar pictorial temperament or constitution, in which, while it may possibly be ignorant of true
anatomical proportions, all things whatever, all poetry, all
ideas however abstract or obscure, float up as visible scene
or image: it is the *coloring*—that weaving of light, as of
just perceptible gold threads, through the dress, the flesh,
the atmosphere, in Titian's *Lace-girl,* that staining of the
whole fabric of the thing with a new, delightful physical
quality. This *drawing,* then—the arabesque traced in the
air by Tintoretto's flying figures, by Titian's forest
branches; this coloring—the magic conditions of light and
hue in the atmosphere of Titian's *Lace-girl,* or Rubens's
Descent from the Cross: these essential pictorial qualities
must first of all delight the sense, delight it as directly and
sensuously as a fragment of Venetian glass; and through
this delight alone become the vehicle of whatever poetry
or science may lie beyond them in the intention of the
composer. In its primary aspect, a great picture has no
more definite message for us than an accidental play of
sunlight and shadow for a few moments on the wall or
floor: is itself, in truth, a space of such fallen light, caught
as the colors are in an Eastern carpet, but refined upon,
and dealt with more subtly and exquisitely than by nature
itself. And this primary and essential condition fulfilled,
we may trace the coming of poetry into painting, by fine
gradations upward; from Japanese fan painting, for instance, where we get, first, only abstract color; then, just
a little interfused sense of the poetry of flowers; then,
sometimes, perfect flower painting; and so, onward, until
in Titian we have, as his poetry in the *Ariadne,* so actually
a touch of true childlike humor in the diminutive, quaint
figure with its silk gown, which ascends the temple stairs,
in his picture of the *Presentation of the Virgin,* at Venice.

But although each art has thus its own specific order of
impressions, and an untranslatable charm, while a just
apprehension of the ultimate differences of the arts is the
beginning of aesthetic criticism; yet it is noticeable that,

in its special mode of handling its given material, each art may be observed to pass into the condition of some other art, by what German critics term an *Anders-streben*—a partial alienation from its own limitations, through which the arts are able, not indeed to supply the place of each other, but reciprocally to lend each other new forces.

Thus some of the most delightful music seems to be always approaching to figure, to pictorial definition. Architecture, again, though it has its own laws—laws esoteric enough, as the true architect knows only too well—yet sometimes aims at fulfilling the conditions of a picture, as in the Arena chapel; or of sculpture, as in the flawless unity of Giotto's tower at Florence; and often finds a true poetry, as in those strangely twisted staircases of the châteaux of the country of the Loire, as if it were intended that among their odd turnings the actors in a theatrical mode of life might pass each other unseen; there being a poetry also of memory and of the mere effect of time, by which architecture often profits greatly. Thus, again, sculpture aspires out of the hard limitation of pure form toward color, or its equivalent; poetry also, in many ways, finding guidance from the other arts, the analogy between a Greek tragedy and a work of Greek sculpture, between a sonnet and a relief, of French poetry generally with the art of engraving, being more than mere figures of speech; and all the arts in common aspiring toward the principle of music; music being the typical, or ideally consummate art, the object of the great *Anders-streben* of all art, of all that is artistic, or partakes of artistic qualities.

All art constantly aspires toward the condition of music. For while in all other kinds of art it is possible to distinguish the matter from the form, and the understanding can always make this distinction, yet it is the constant effort of art to obliterate it. That the mere matter of a poem, for instance, its subject, namely, its given incidents or situation—that the mere matter of a picture, the actual circumstances of an event, the actual topography of a landscape—should be nothing without the form, the spirit, of the handling; that this form, this mode of handling, should become an end in itself, should penetrate every part of the matter: this is what all art constantly strives after, and achieves in different degrees.

This abstract language becomes clear enough, if we

think of actual examples. In an actual landscape we see a long white road, lost suddenly on the hill verge. That is the matter of one of the etchings of M. Alphonse Legros: only, in this etching, it is informed by an indwelling solemnity of expression, seen upon it or half seen, within the limits of an exceptional moment, or caught from his own mood perhaps, but which he maintains as the very essence of the thing, throughout his work. Sometimes a momentary tint of stormy light may invest a homely or too familiar scene with a character which might well have been drawn from the deep places of the imagination. Then we might say that this particular effect of light, this sudden inweaving of gold thread through the texture of the haystack, and the poplars, and the grass, gives the scene artistic qualities; that it is like a picture. And such tricks of circumstance are commonest in landscape which has little salient character of its own; because, in such scenery, all the material details are so easily absorbed by that informing expression of passing light, and elevated, throughout their whole extent, to a new and delightful effect by it. And hence the superiority, for most conditions of the picturesque, of a riverside in France to a Swiss valley, because, on the French riverside, mere topography, the simple material, counts for so little, and, all being very pure, untouched, and tranquil in itself, mere light and shade have such easy work in modulating it to one dominant tone. The Venetian landscape, on the other hand, has in its material conditions much which is hard, or harshly definite; but the masters of the Venetian school have shown themselves little burdened by them. Of its Alpine background they retain certain abstracted elements only, of cool color and tranquillizing line; and they use its actual details, the brown windy turrets, the straw-colored fields, the forest arabesques, but as the notes of a music which duly accompanies the presence of their men and women, presenting us with the spirit of essence only of a certain sort of landscape—a country of the pure reason or half-imaginative memory.

Poetry, again, works with words addressed in the first instance to the pure intelligence; and it deals, most often, with a definite subject or situation. Sometimes it may find a noble and quite legitimate function in the conveyance of moral or political aspiration, as often in the poetry of

Victor Hugo. In such instances it is easy enough for the understanding to distinguish between the matter and the form, however much the matter, the subject, the element which is addressed to the mere intelligence, has been penetrated by the informing, artistic spirit. But the ideal types of poetry are those in which this distinction is reduced to its *minimum;* so that lyrical poetry, precisely because in it we are least able to detach the matter from the form, without a deduction of something from that matter itself, is, at least artistically, the highest and most complete form of poetry. And the very perfection of such poetry often seems to depend, in part, on a certain suppression or vagueness of mere subject, so that the meaning reached us through ways not distinctly traceable by the understanding, as in some of the most imaginative compositions of William Blake, and often in Shakespeare's songs, as pre-eminently in that song of Mariana's page in *Measure for Measure,* in which the kindling force and poetry of the whole play seems to pass for a moment into an actual strain of music.

And this principle holds good of all things that partake in any degree of artistic qualities, of the furniture of our houses, and of dress, for instance, of life itself, of gesture and speech, and the details of daily intercourse; these also, for the wise, being susceptible of a suavity and charm, caught from the way in which they are done, which gives them a worth in themselves, wherein, indeed, lies what is valuable and justly attractive, in what is called the fashion of a time, which elevates the trivialities of speech, and manner, and dress, into ends in themselves, and gives them a mysterious grace and attractiveness in the doing of them.

Art, then, is thus always striving to be independent of the mere intelligence, to become a matter of pure perception, to get rid of its responsibilities to its subject or material; the ideal examples of poetry and painting being those in which the constituent elements of the composition are so welded together, that the material or subject no longer strikes the intellect only; nor the form, the eye or the ear only; but form and matter, in their union or identity, present one single effect to the "imaginative reason," that complex faculty for which every thought and feeling is twin-born with its sensible analogue or symbol.

It is the art of music which most completely realizes

this artistic ideal, this perfect identification of matter and form. In its consummate moments, the end is not distinct from the means, the form from the matter, the subject from the expression; they inhere in and completely saturate each other; and to it, therefore, to the condition of its perfect moments, all the arts may be supposed constantly to tend and aspire. Music, then, and not poetry, as is so often supposed, is the true type or measure of perfected art. Therefore, although each art has its incommunicable element, its untranslatable order of impressions, its unique mode of reaching the "imaginative reason," yet the arts may be represented as continually struggling after the law or principle of music, to a condition which music alone completely realizes; and one of the chief functions of aesthetic criticism, dealing with the products of art, new or old, is to estimate the degree in which each of those products approaches, in this sense, to musical law.

By no school of painters have the necessary limitations of the art of painting been so unerringly though instinctively apprehended, and the essence of what is pictorial in a picture so justly conceived, as by the school of Venice; and the train of thought suggested in what has been now said is, perhaps, a not unfitting introduction to a few pages about Giorgione, who, though much has been taken by recent criticism from what was reputed to be his work, yet, more entirely than any other painter, sums up, in what we know of himself and his art, the spirit of the Venetian school.

The beginnings of Venetian painting link themselves to the last, stiff, half-barbaric splendors of Byzantine decoration, and are but the introduction into the crust of marble and gold on the walls of the Duomo of Murano, or of Saint Mark's, of a little more of human expression. And throughout the course of its later development, always subordinate to architectual effect, the work of the Venetian school never escaped from the influence of its beginnings. Unassisted, and therefore unperplexed, by naturalism, religious mysticism, philosophical theories, it had no Giotto, no Angelico, no Botticelli. Exempt from the stress of thought and sentiment, which taxed so severely the resources of the generations of Florentine artists, those earlier Venetian painters, down to Carpaccio and the Bellini, seem never for a moment to have been tempted even to lose sight of the scope of their art in its strictness, or to forget that painting must be before all things decorative, a thing for the eye, a space of color on the wall, only more dexterously blent than the marking of its precious stone or the chance interchange of sun and shade upon it—this, to begin and end with—whatever higher matter of thought, or poetry, or religious revery might play its part therein, between. At last, with final mastery of all the technical secrets of his art, and with somewhat more than "a spark of the divine fire" to his share, comes Giorgione. He is the inventor of *genre,* of those easily movable pictures which serve neither for uses of devotion, nor of allegorical or historic teaching—little groups of real men and women, amid congruous furniture or landscape—morsels of actual life, conversation or music or play, but refined upon or idealized, till they come to seem like glimpses of life from afar. Those spaces of more cunningly blent color, obediently filling their places, hitherto, in a mere architectural scheme, Giorgione detaches from the wall. He frames them by the hands of some skillful carver, so that people may move them readily and take with them where they go, as one might a poem in manuscript, or a musical instrument, to be used, at will, as a means of self-education, stimulus or solace, coming like an animated presence, into one's cabinet, to enrich the air as with some choice aroma, and, like persons, live with us, for a day or a lifetime. Of all art such as this, art which has played so large a part in men's culture since that time, Giorgione is the initiator. Yet in him too that old Venetian clearness or justice, in the apprehension of the essential limitations of the pictorial art, is still undisturbed, and while he interfuses his painted work with a high-strung sort of poetry, caught directly from a singularly rich and high-strung sort of life, yet in his selection of subject, or phase of subject, in the subordination of mere subject to pictorial design, to the main purpose of a picture, he is typical of that aspiration of all the arts toward music, which I have endeavored to explain—toward the perfect identification of matter and form.

Born so near to Titian, though a little before him, that these two companion pupils of the aged Giovanni Bellini may almost be called contemporaries, Giorgione stands to

Titian in something like the relationship of Sordello to Dante, in Browning's poem. Titian, when he leaves Bellini, becomes, in turn, the pupil of Giorgione; he lives in constant labor more than sixty years after Giorgione is in his grave; and with such fruit, that hardly one of the greater towns of Europe is without some fragment of his work. But the slightly older man, with his so limited actual product (what remains to us of it seeming, when narrowly explained, to reduce itself to almost one picture, like Sordello's one fragment of lovely verse), yet expresses, in elementary motive and principle, that spirit—itself the final acquisition of all the long endeavors of Venetian art— which Titian spreads over his whole life's activity.

And, as we might expect, something fabulous and illusive has always mingled itself in the brilliancy of Giorgione's fame. The exact relationship to him of many works —drawings, portraits, painted idylls—often fascinating enough, which in various collections went by his name, was from the first uncertain. Still, six or eight famous pictures at Dresden, Florence and the Louvre, were with no doubt attributed to him, and in these, if anywhere, something of the splendor of the old Venetian humanity seemed to have been preserved. But of those six or eight famous pictures it is now known that only one is certainly from Giorgione's hand. The accomplished science of the subject has come at last, and, as in other instances, has not made the past more real for us, but assured us only that we possess less of it than we seemed to possess. Much of the work on which Giorgione's immediate fame depended, work done for instantaneous effect, in all probability passed away almost within his own age, like the frescoes on the façade of the Fondaco dei Tedeschi at Venice, some crimson traces of which, however, still give a strange additional touch of splendor to the scene of the Rialto. And then there is a barrier or borderland, a period about the middle of the sixteenth century, in passing through which the tradition miscarries, and the true outlines of Giorgione's work and person are obscured. It became fashionable for wealthy lovers of art, with no critical standard of authenticity, to collect so-called works of Giorgione, and a multitude of imitations came into circulation. And now, in the "new Vasari," * the great

* Crowe and Cavalcaselle: *History of Painting in North Italy.*

traditional reputation, woven with so profuse demand on men's admiration, has been scrutinized thread by thread; and what remains of the most vivid and stimulating of Venetian masters, a live flame, as it seemed, in those old shadowy times, has been reduced almost to a name by his most recent critics.

Yet enough remains to explain why the legend grew up above the name, why the name attached itself, in many instances, to the bravest work of other men. The *Concert* in the Pitti Palace, in which a monk, with cowl and tonsure, touches the keys of a harpsichord, while a clerk, placed behind him, grasps the handle of the viol, and a third, with cap and plume, seems to wait upon the true interval for beginning to sing, is undoubtedly Giorgione's. The outline of the lifted finger, the trace of the plume, the very threads of the fine linen, which fasten themselves on the memory, in the moment before they are lost altogether in that calm unearthly glow, the skill which has caught the waves of wandering sound, and fixed them forever on the lips and hands—these are indeed the master's own; and the criticism which, while dismissing so much hitherto believed to be Giorgione's, has established the claims of this one picture, has left it among the most precious things in the world of art.

It is noticeable that the "distinction" of this *Concert,* its sustained evenness of perfection, alike in design, in execution, and in choice of personal type, becomes for the "new Vasari" the standard of Giorgione's genuine work. Finding here enough to explain his influence, and the true seal of mastery, its authors assign to Pellegrino da San Daniele the *Holy Family* in the Louvre, for certain points in which it comes short of this standard, but which will hardly diminish the spectator's enjoyment of a singular charm of liquid air, with which the whole picture seems instinct, filling the eyes and lips, the very garments, of its sacred personages, with some wind-searched brightness and energy; of which fine air the blue peak, clearly defined in the distance, is, as it were, the visible pledge. Similarly, another favorite picture in the Louvre, the subject of a delightful sonnet by a poet * whose own painted work often comes to mind as one ponders over these precious things—the *Fête Champêtre,* is assigned to an imitator of

* Dante Gabriel Rossetti.

Sebastian del Piombo; and the *Tempest,* in the Academy at Venice (a slighter loss, perhaps, though not without its pleasant effect of clearing weather, toward the left, its one untouched morsel), to Paris Bordone, or perhaps to "some advanced craftsman of the sixteenth century." From the gallery at Dresden, the *Knight Embracing a Lady,* where the knight's broken gauntlets seem to mark some well-known pause in a story we would willingly hear the rest of, is conceded to "a Brescian hand," and *Jacob Meeting Rachel* to a pupil of Palma; and whatever their charm, we are called on to give up the *Ordeal,* and the *Finding of Moses* with its jewellike pools of water, perhaps to Bellini.

Nor has the criticism, which thus so freely diminishes the number of his authentic works, added anything important to the well-known outline of the life and personality of the man: only, it has fixed one or two dates, one or two circumstances, a little more exactly. Giorgione was born before the year 1477, and spent his childhood at Castelfranco, where the last crags of the Venetian Alps break down romantically, with something of parklike grace, to the plain. A natural child of the family of the Barbarelli by a peasant girl of Vedelago, he finds his way early into the circle of notable persons—people of courtesy; and becomes initiated into those differences of personal type, manner, and even of dress, which are best understood there—that "distinction" of the *Concert* of the Pitti Palace. Not far from his home lives Catherine of Cornara, formerly Queen of Cyprus; and, up in the towers which still remain, Tuzio Costanzo, the famous *condottiére*—a picturesque remnant of medieval manners, amid a civilization rapidly changing. Giorgione paints their portraits; and when Tuzio's son, Matteo, dies in early youth, adorns in his memory a chapel in the church of Castelfranco, painting on this occasion, perhaps, the altarpiece, foremost among his authentic works, still to be seen there, with the figure of the warrior saint, Liberale, of which the original little study in oil, with the delicately gleaming, silver-grey armor, is one of the greater treasures of the National Gallery. In that figure, as in some other knightly personages attributed to him, people have supposed the likeness of the painter's own presumably gracious presence. Thither, at last, he is himself brought home from Venice, early dead, but celebrated. It happened, about his thirty-fourth year, that in one of those parties at which he entertained his friends with music, he met a certain lady of whom he became greatly enamored, and "they rejoiced greatly," says Vasari, "the one and the other, in their loves." And two quite different legends concerning it agree in this, that it was through this lady he came by his death; Ridolfi relating that, being robbed of her by one of his pupils, he died of grief at the double treason; Vasari, that she being secretly stricken of the plague, and he making his visits to her as usual, he took the sickness from her mortally, along with her kisses, and so briefly departed.

But, although the number of Giorgione's extant works has been thus limited by recent criticism, all is not done when the real and the traditional elements in what concerns him have been discriminated; for, in what is connected with a great name, much that is not real is often very stimulating, and, for the aesthetic philosopher, therefore, over and above the real Giorgione and his authentic extant works, there remains the *Giorgionesque* also—an influence, a spirit or type in art, active in men so different as those to whom many of his supposed works are really assignable—a veritable school, in fact, grew together out of all those fascinating works rightly or wrongly attributed to him; out of many copies from, or variations on him, by unknown or uncertain workmen, whose drawings and designs were, for various reasons, prized as his; out of the immediate impression he made upon his contemporaries, and with which he continued in men's minds; out of many traditions of subject and treatment, which really descend from him to our own time, and by retracing which we fill out the original image; Giorgione thus becoming a sort of impersonation of Venice itself, its projected reflex or ideal, all that was intense or desirable in its crystallizing about the memory of this wonderful young man.

And now, finally, let me illustrate some of the characteristics of this *School of Giorgione,* as we may call it, which, for most of us, notwithstanding all that negative criticism of the "new Vasari," will still identify itself with those famous pictures at Florence, at Dresden and Paris. A certain artistic ideal is there defined for us—the conception of a peculiar aim and procedure in art, which we may understand as the *Giorgionesque,* wherever we find it, whether in Venetian work generally, or in work of our own time—and of which the *Concert,* that undoubted work of Giorgione in the Pitti Palace, is the typical instance, and a pledge authenticating the connection of the school with the master.

I have spoken of a certain interpenetration of the matter or subject of a work of art with the form of it, a condition realized absolutely only in music, as the condition to which every form of art is perpetually aspiring. In the art of painting, the attainment of this ideal condition, this perfect interpenetration of the subject with the elements of color and design, depends, of course, in great measure, on dexterous choice of that subject, or phase of subject; and such choice is one of the secrets of Giorgione's school. It is the school of *genre,* and employs itself mainly with "painted idylls," but, in the production of this pictorial poetry, exercises a wonderful tact in the selecting of such matter as lends itself most readily and entirely to pictorial form, to complete expression by drawing and color. For although its productions are painted poems, they belong to a sort of poetry which tells itself without an articulated story. The master is pre-eminent for the resolution, the ease and quickness, with which he reproduces instantaneous motion—the lacing on of armor, with the head bent back so stately—the fainting lady—the embrace, rapid as the kiss, caught with death itself from dying lips—the momentary conjunction of mirrors and polished armor and still water, by which all the sides of a solid image are exhibited at once, solving that casuistical question whether painting can present an object as completely as sculpture. The sudden act, the rapid transition of thought, the passing expression—this he arrests with that vivacity which Vasari has attributed to him, *il fuoco Giorgionesco,* as he terms it. Now it is part of the ideality of the highest sort of dramatic poetry, that it presents us with a kind of profoundly significant and animated instants, a mere gesture, a look, a smile, perhaps—some brief and wholly concrete moment—into which, however, all the motives, all the interests and effects of a long history, have condensed themselves, and which seem to absorb past and future in an intense consciousness of the present. Such ideal instants the school of Giorgione selects, with its admirable tact, from that feverish, tumultuously colored world of the old citizens of Venice—exquisite pauses in time, in which, arrested thus, we seem to be spectators of all the fullness of existence, and which are like some consummate extract or quintessence of life.

It is to the law or condition of music, as I said, that all art like this is really aspiring; and, in the school of Giorgione, the perfect moments of music itself, the making or hearing of music, song or its accompaniment, are themselves prominent as subjects. On that background of the silence of Venice, so impressive to the modern visitor, the world of Italian music was then forming. In choice of subject, as in all besides, the *Concert* of the Pitti Palace is typical of everything that Giorgione, himself an admirable musician, touched with his influence; and in sketch or finished picture, in various collections, we may follow it through many intricate variations—men fainting at music; music heard at the poolside while people fish, or mingled with the sound of the pitcher in the well, or heard across running water, or among the flocks; the tuning of instruments; people with intent faces, as if listening, like those described by Plato in an ingenious passage of the *Republic,* to detect the smallest interval of musical sound, the smallest undulation in the air, or feeling for music in thought on a stringless instrument, ear and finger refining themselves infinitely, in the appetite for sweet sound; a momentary touch of an instrument in the twilight, as one passes through some unfamiliar room, in a chance company.

In these then, the favorite incidents of Giorgione's school, music or musiclike intervals in our existence, life itself is conceived as a sort of listening—listening to music, to the reading of Bandello's novels, to the sound of water, to time as it flies. Often such moments are really our moments of play, and we are surprised at the unexpected blessedness of what may seem our least important part of time; not merely because play is in many instances that to which people really apply their own best powers, but also because at such times, the stress of our servile, everyday attentiveness being relaxed, the happier powers in things without are permitted free passage, and have their way with us. And so, from music, the school of Giorgione passes often to the play which is like music; to those masques in which men avowedly do but play at real life, like children dressing up, disguised in the strange old Italian dresses, particolored, or fantastic with embroidery and furs, of which the master was so curious a designer, and which, above all the spotless white linen at wrist and throat, he painted so dexterously.

But when people are happy in this thirsty land water will not be far off; and in the school of Giorgione, the presence of water—the well, or marble-rimmed pool, the drawing or pouring of water, as the woman pours it from a pitcher with her jeweled hand in the *Fête Champêtre,* listening, perhaps, to the cool sound as it falls, blent with the music of the pipes—is as characteristic, and almost as suggestive, as that of music itself. And the landscape feels, and is glad of it also—a landscape full of clearness, of the effects of water, of fresh rain newly passed through the air, and collected into the grassy channels; the air, too, in the school of Giorgione, seems as vivid as the people who breathe it, and literally empyrean, all impurities being burnt out of it, and no taint, no floating particle of anything but its own proper elements allowed to subsist within it.

Its scenery is such as in England we call "park scenery," with some elusive refinement felt about the rustic buildings, the choice grass, the grouped trees, the undulations deftly economized for graceful effect. Only, in Italy all natural things are as it were woven through and through with gold thread, even the cypress revealing it among the folds of its blackness. And it is with gold dust, or gold thread, that these Venetian painters seem to work, spinning its fine filaments, through the solemn human flesh, away into the white plastered walls of the thatched huts. The harsher details of the mountains recede to a harmonious distance, the one peak of rich blue above the horizon remaining but as the visible warrant of that due coolness which is all we need ask here of the Alps, with their dark rains and streams. Yet what real, airy space, as the eye passes from level to level, through the long-drawn valley in which Jacob embraces Rachel among the flocks! Nowhere is there a truer instance of that balance, that modulated unison of landscape and persons—of the human image and its accessories—already noticed as characteristic of the Venetian school, so that, in it, neither personage nor scenery is ever a mere pretext for the other.

Something like this seems to me to be the *vraie vérité* about Giorgione, if I may adopt a serviceable expression, by which the French recognize those more liberal and durable impressions which, in respect of any really considerable person or subject, anything that has at all intricately occupied men's attention, lie beyond, and must supplement, the narrower range of the strictly ascertained facts about it. In this, Giorgione is but an illustration of a valuable general caution we may abide by in all criticism. As regards Giorgione himself, we have indeed to take note of all those negations and exceptions, by which, at first sight, a "new Vasari" seems merely to have confused our apprehension of a delightful object, to have explained away in our inheritance from past time what seemed of high value there. Yet it is not with a full understanding even of those exceptions that one can leave off just at this point. Properly qualified, such exceptions are but a salt of genuineness in our knowledge; and beyond all those strictly ascertained facts, we must take note of that indirect influence by which one like Giorgione, for instance, enlarges his permanent efficacy and really makes himself felt in our culture. In a just impression of that, is the essential truth, the *vraie vérité,* concerning him.

JOACHIM DU BELLAY

IN the middle of the sixteenth century, when the spirit of the Renaissance was everywhere, and people had begun to look back with distaste on the works of the Middle Ages, the old Gothic manner had still one chance more, in borrowing something from the rival which was about to supplant it. In this way there was produced, chiefly in France, a new and peculiar phase of taste with qualities and a charm of its own, blending the somewhat attenuated grace of Italian ornament with the general outlines of Northern design. It created the Château de Gaillon, as you may still see it in the delicate engravings of Isräel Silvestre —a Gothic donjon veiled faintly by a surface of dainty Italian traceries—Chenonceaux, Blois, Chambord, and the church of Brou. In painting, there came from Italy workmen like Maître Roux and the masters of the school of Fontainebleau, to have their later Italian voluptuousness attempered by the naive and silvery qualities of the native style; and it was characteristic of these painters that they were most successful in painting on glass, an art so essentially medieval. Taking it up where the Middle Ages had left it, they found their whole work among the last subtleties of color and line; and keeping within the true limits of their material, they got quite a new order of effects from it, and felt their way to refinements on color never dreamed of by those older workmen, the glass painters of Chartres or Le Mans. What is called the Renaissance in France is thus not so much the introduction of a wholly new taste ready-made from Italy, but rather the finest and subtlest phase of the Middle Ages itself, its last fleeting splendor and temperate Saint Martin's summer. In poetry, the Gothic spirit in France had produced a thousand songs; and in the Renaissance, French poetry too did but borrow something to blend with a native growth, and the poems of Ronsard, with their ingenuity, their delicately figured surfaces, their slightness, their fanciful combination of rhyme, are but the correlative of the traceries of the house of Jacques Coeur at Bourges, or the Maison de Justice at Rouen.

There was indeed something in the native French taste naturally akin to that Italian finesse. The characteristic of French work had always been a certain nicety—*une netteté remarquable d'exécution*. In the paintings of François Clouet, for example, or rather of the Clouets—for there was a whole family of them—painters remarkable for their resistance to Italian influences, there is a silveriness of color and a clearness of expression which distinguish them very definitely from their Flemish neighbors, Hemling or the Van Eycks. And this nicety is not less characteristic of old French poetry. A light, aerial delicacy, a simple elegance, *une netteté remarquable d'exécution*— these are essential characteristics alike of Villon's poetry, and of the *Hours of Anne of Brittany*. They are characteristic too of a hundred French Gothic carvings and traceries. Alike in the old Gothic cathedrals, and in their counterpart, the old Gothic *chansons de geste,* the rough and ponderous mass becomes, as if by passing for a moment into happier conditions, or through a more gracious stratum of air, graceful and refined, like the carved ferneries on the granite church at Folgoat, or the lines which describe the fair priestly hands of Bishop Turpin, in the *Song of Roland;* although below both alike there is a fund of mere Gothic strength, or heaviness.

And Villon's songs and Clouet's painting are like these. It is the higher touch making itself felt here and there, betraying itself, like nobler blood in a lower stock, by a fine line or gesture or expression, the turn of a wrist, the tapering of a finger. In Ronsard's time that rougher element seemed likely to predominate. No one can turn over the pages of Rabelais without feeling how much need there was of softening, of castigation. To effect this softening is the object of the revolution in poetry which is connected with Ronsard's name. Casting about for the means of thus refining upon and saving the character of French literature, he accepted that influx of Renaissance taste, which, leaving the buildings, the language, the art, the poetry of France, at bottom, what they were, old French Gothic still, gilds their surfaces with a strange, delightful, foreign aspect, passing over all that Northern land neither deeper nor more permanent than a chance effect of light. He reinforces, he doubles the French *netteté* by Italian finesse. Thereupon, nearly all the force and all the seriousness of French work disappear; only the elegance, the aerial touch, the perfect manner remain. But this elegance, this manner, this *netteté d'exécution* are consummate, and have an unmistakable aesthetic value.

So the old French chanson, which, like the old Northern Gothic ornament, though it sometimes refined itself into a sort of weird elegance, was often, in its essence, something rude and formless, became in the hands of Ronsard a Pindaric ode. He gave it structure, a sustained system, strophe and antistrophe, and taught it a changefulness and variety of meter which keep the curiosity always excited, so that the very aspect of it, as it lies written on the page, carries the eye lightly onward, and of which this is a good instance:

> *Avril, la grace, et le ris*
> *De Cypris,*
> *Le flair et la douce haleine;*
> *Avril, le parfum des dieux,*

Qui, des cieux,
Sentent l'odeur de la plaine;

C'est toy, courtois et gentil,
Qui d'exil
Retire ces passageres,
Ces arondelles qui vont,
Et qui sont
Du printemps les messageres.*

That, is not by Ronsard, but by Remy Belleau, for Ronsard soon came to have a school. Six other poets threw in their lot with him in his literary revolution—this Remy Belleau, Antoine de Bäif, Pontus de Tyard, Estienne Jodelle, Jean Daurat, and lastly Joachim du Bellay; and with that strange love of emblems which is characteristic of the time, which covered all the works of Francis the First with the salamander, and all the works of Henry the Second with the double crescent, and all the works of Anne of Brittany with the knotted cord, they called themselves the Pléiade; seven in all, although as happens with the celestial Pleiad, if you scrutinize this constellation of poets more carefully you may find there a great number of minor stars.

The first note of this literary revolution was struck by Joachim du Bellay in a little tract written at the early age of twenty-four, which coming to us through three centuries seems of yesterday, so full is it of those delicate critical distinctions which are sometimes supposed peculiar to

* April, with thy gracious wiles,
    Like the smiles,
Smiles of Venus; and thy breath
Like her breath, the gods' delight,
    (From their height
They take the happy air beneath;)

It is thou that, of thy grace,
    From their place
In the far-off isles dost bring
Swallows over earth and sea,
    Glad to be
Messengers of thee, and Spring.

(Stanzas 6 and 7 of "April" in *Ballads of Old France*, by Andrew Lang.)

modern writers. The piece has for its title *La Deffense et illustration de la langue francoyse;* and its problem is how to illustrate or ennoble the French language, to give it luster. We are accustomed to speak of the varied critical and creative movement of the fifteenth and sixteenth centuries as the Renaissance and because we have a single name for it we may sometimes fancy that there was more unity in the thing itself than there really was. Even the Reformation, that other great movement of the fifteenth and sixteenth centuries, had far less unity, far less of combined action, than is at first sight supposed; and the Renaissance was infinitely less united, less conscious of combined action, than the Reformation. But if anywhere the Renaissance became conscious, as a German philosopher might say, if ever it was understood as a systematic movement by those who took part in it, it is in this little book of Joachim du Bellay's, which it is impossible to read without feeling the excitement, the animation, of change, of discovery. *La prose,* says M. Sainte-Beuve, *chose remarquable et à l'inverse des autres langues, a toujours eu le pas chez nous, sur notre poésie.* Du Bellay's prose is perfectly transparent, flexible and chaste. In many ways it is a more characteristic example of the culture of the Pléiade than any of its verse; and those who love the whole movement of which the Pléiade is a part, for a weird foreign grace in it, and may be looking about for a true specimen of it, cannot have a better than Joachim du Bellay and this little treatise of his.

Du Bellay's object is to adjust the existing French culture to the rediscovered classical culture; and in discussing this problem, and developing the theories of the Pléiade, he has lighted upon many principles of permanent truth and applicability. There were some who despaired of the French language altogether, who thought it naturally incapable of the fullness and elegance of Greek and Latin *(cette élégance et copie qui est en la langue Greque et Romaine)*—that science could be adequately discussed, and poetry nobly written, only in the dead languages. *Those who speak thus,* says Du Bellay, *make me think of those relics which one may only see through a little pane of glass, and must not touch with one's hands. That is what these people do with all branches of culture, which they keep shut up in Greek and Latin books, not permit-*

ting one to see them otherwise, or transport them out of dead words into those which are alive, and wing their way daily through the mouths of men. Languages, he says again, *are not born like plants and trees, some naturally feeble and sickly, others healthy and strong and apter to bear the weight of men's conceptions, but all their virtue is generated in the world of choice and men's freewill concerning them. Therefore, I cannot blame too strongly the rashness of some of our countrymen, who being anything rather than Greeks or Latins, depreciate and reject with more than stoical disdain everything written in French; nor can I express my surprise at the odd opinion of some learned men who think that our vulgar tongue is wholly incapable of erudition and good literature.*

It was an age of translations. Du Bellay himself translated two books of the *Aeneid,* and other poetry, old and new, and there were some who thought that the translation of the classical literature was the true means of *ennobling* the French language—*nous favorisons toujours les étrangers.* Du Bellay moderates their expectations. *I do not believe that one can learn the right use of them*—he is speaking of figures and ornament in language—*from translations, because it is impossible to reproduce them with the same grace with which the original author used them. For each language has, I know not what peculiarity of its own; and if you force yourself to express the naturalness* (le näif) *of this in another language, observing the law of translation, which is, not to expatiate beyond the limits of the author himself, your words will be constrained, cold and ungraceful.* Then he fixes the test of all good translation: *To prove this, read me Demosthenes and Homer in Latin, Cicero and Virgil in French, and see whether they produce in you the same affections which you experience in reading those authors in the original.*

In this effort to ennoble the French language, to give it grace, number, perfection, and as painters do to their pictures, *cette dernière main que nous désirons,* what Du Bellay is pleading for is his mother tongue, the language, that is, in which one will have the utmost degree of what is moving and passionate. He recognized of what force the music and dignity of languages are, how they enter into the inmost part of things; and in pleading for the cultivation of the French language, he is pleading for no merely scholastic interest, but for freedom, impulse, reality, not in literature merely, but in daily communion of speech. After all, it was impossible to have this impulse in Greek and Latin, dead languages, *péris et mises en reliquaires de livres*. By aid of this poor *plante et vergette* of the French language, he must speak delicately, movingly, if he is ever to speak so at all; that, or none, must be for him the medium of what he calls, in one of his great phrases, *le discours fatal des choses mondaines;* and it is his patriotism not to despair of it; he sees it already, *parfait en toute élégance et venuste de paroles*.

Du Bellay was born in the disastrous year 1525, the year of the battle of Pavia, and the captivity of Francis the First. His parents died early, and to him, as the younger son, his mother's little estate, ce petit Liré, the beloved place of his birth, descended. He was brought up by a brother only a little older than himself; and left to themselves the two boys passed their lives in daydreams of military glory. Their education was neglected; "the time of my youth," says Du Bellay, "was lost, like the flower which no shower waters, and no hand cultivates." He was just twenty years old when the elder brother died, leaving Joachim to be the guardian of his child. It was with regret, with a shrinking feeling of incapacity, that he took upon him the burden of this responsibility. Hitherto he had looked forward to the profession of a soldier, hereditary in his family. But at this time a sickness attacked him which brought him cruel sufferings, and seemed likely to be mortal. It was then for the first time that he read the Greek and Latin poets. These studies came too late to make him what he so much desired to be, a trifler in Greek and Latin verse, like so many others of his time now forgotten; instead, they made him a lover of his own homely native tongue, that poor *plante et vergette* of the French language. It was through this fortunate shortcoming in his education that he became national and modern; and he learned afterward to look back on that wild garden of his youth with only a half regret. A certain Cardinal du Bellay was the successful member of the family, a man often employed in high official affairs. It was to him that the thoughts of Joachim turned when it became necessary to choose a profession, and in 1552 he accompanied the Cardinal to Rome. He remained there nearly five years, burdened with the weight of affairs, and languishing with homesickness. Yet it was under these circumstances that his genius yielded its best fruits. From Rome, which to most men of an imaginative temperament like his would have yielded so many pleasurable sensations, with all the curiosities of the Renaissance still fresh there, his thoughts went back painfully, longingly, to the country of the Loire, with its wide expanses of waving corn, its homely pointed roofs of gray slate, and its faroff scent of the sea. He reached home at last, but only to die there, quite suddenly, one wintry day, at the early age of thirty-five.

Much of Du Bellay's poetry illustrates rather the age and school to which he belonged than his own temper and genius. As with the writings of Ronsard and the other poets of the Pléiade, its interest depends not so much on the impress of individual genius upon it, as on the circumstance that it was once poetry à la mode, that it is part of the manner of a time, a time which made much of manner, and carried it to a high degree of perfection. It is one of the decorations of an age which threw much of its energy into the work of decoration. We feel a pensive pleasure in seeing these faded decorations, and observing how a group of actual men and women pleased themselves long ago. Ronsard's poems are a kind of epitome of his age. Of one side of that age, it is true, of the strenuous, the progressive, the serious movement, which was then going on, there is little; but of the catholic side, the losing side, the forlorn hope, hardly a figure is absent. The Queen of Scots, at whose desire Ronsard published his odes, reading him in her northern prison, felt that he was bringing back to her the true flavor of her early days in the court of Catherine at the Louvre, with its exotic Italian gaieties. Those who disliked that poetry, disliked it because they found that age itself distasteful. The poetry of Malherbe came, with its sustained style and weighty sentiment, but with nothing that set people singing; and the lovers of such poetry saw in the poetry of the Pléiade only the latest trumpery of the Middle Ages. But the time came also when the school of Malherbe had had its day; and the Romanticists, who in their eagerness for excitement, for strange music and imagery, went back to the works of the Middle Ages, accepted the Pléiade too with the rest; and in the new Middle Ages which their genius has evoked, the poetry of the Pléiade has found its place. At first, with Malherbe, you may find it, like the architecture, the whole mode of life, the very dresses of that time, fantastic, faded, rococo. But if you look long enough to understand it, to conceive its sentiment, you will find that those wanton lines have a spirit guiding their caprices. For there is *style* there; one temper has shaped the whole; and everything that has style, that has been done as no other man or age could have done it, as it could never, for all our trying, be done again, has its true value and interest. Let us dwell upon it for a moment, and try to gather from it that *fleur particulier,* that special flower, which Ronsard himself tells us every garden has.

It is poetry not for the people, but for a confined circle, for courtiers, great lords and erudite persons, people who desire to be humored, to gratify a certain refined voluptuousness they have in them. Ronsard loves, or dreams that he loves, a rare and peculiar type of beauty, *la petite pucelle Angevine,* with blonde hair and dark eyes. But he has the ambition not only of being a courtier and a lover, but a great scholar also; he is anxious about orthography, about the letter *è Grecque,* the true spelling of Latin names in French writing, and the restoration of the *i voyelle en sa première liberté.* His poetry is full of quaint, remote learning. He is just a little pedantic, true always to his own express judgment, that to be natural is not enough for one who in poetry desires to produce work worthy of immortality. And therewithal a certain number of Greek words, which charmed Ronsard and his circle by their gayness and nicety, and a certain air of foreign elegance about them, crept into the French language; and there were other strange words which the poets of the Pléiade forged for themselves, and which had only an ephemeral existence.

With this was mixed the desire to taste a more exquisite and various music than that of the older French verse, or of the classical poets. The music of the measured, scanned verse of Latin and Greek poetry is one thing; the music of the rhymed, unscanned verse of Villon and the old French poets, the *poésie chantée,* is another. To unite together these two kinds of music in a new school of French poetry, to make verse which should scan and rhyme as well, to search out and harmonize the measure of every syllable, and unite it to the swift, flitting, swallowlike motion of rhyme, to penetrate their poetry with a double music—this was the ambition of the Pléiade. They are insatiable of music, they cannot have enough of it; they desire a music of greater compass perhaps than words can possibly yield, to drain out the last drops of sweetness which a certain note or accent contains.

This eagerness for music is almost the only serious thing in the poetry of the Pléiade; and it was Goudimel, the severe and Protestant Goudimel, who set Ronsard's songs to music. But except in this these poets seem never quite in earnest. The old Greek and Roman mythology, which for the great Italians had been a motive so weighty and severe, becomes with them a mere toy. That "lord of terrible aspect," *Amor,* has become the *petit enfant Amour.* They are full of fine railleries; they delight in diminutives, *ondelette, fontelette, doucelette, Cassandrette.* Their loves are only half real, a vain effort to prolong the imaginative loves of the Middle Ages beyond their natural lifetime. They write love poems for hire. Like the party of people who tell the tales of Boccaccio's *Decameron,* they form a circle which in an age of great troubles, losses, anxieties, amuses itself with art, poetry, intrigue. But they amuse themselves with wonderful elegance; and sometimes their gaiety becomes satiric, for, as they play, real passions insinuate themselves, and at least the reality of death; their dejection at the thought of leaving *le beau séjour du commun jour* is expressed by them with almost wearisome reiteration. But with this sentiment too they are able to trifle; the imagery of death serves for a delicate ornament, and they weave into the airy nothingness of their verses their trite reflections on the vanity of life; just as the grotesques of the charnelhouse nest themselves, together with birds and flowers and the fancies of the pagan mythology, in the traceries of the architecture of that time, which wantons in its delicate arabesques with the images of old age and death.

Ronsard became deaf at sixteen; and it was this which finally determined him to be a man of letters instead of a diplomatist; and it was significant, one might fancy, of a certain premature agedness, and of the tranquil, temperate sweetness appropriate to that, in the school of poetry which he founded. Its charm is that of a thing not vigorous or original, but full of the grace that comes of long study and reiterated refinements, and many steps repeated, and many angles worn down, with an exquisite faintness (*une fadeur exquise*), a certain tenuity and caducity, as for those who can bear nothing vehement or strong; for princes weary of love, like Francis the First, or of pleasure, like Henry the Third, or of action like Henry the Fourth. Its merits are those of the old, grace and finish, perfect in minute detail. For these people are a little jaded, and have a constant desire for a subdued and delicate excitement, to warm their creeping fancy a little. They love a constant change of rhyme in poetry, and in their houses that strange, fantastic interweaving of thin, reedlike lines, which are a kind of rhetoric in architecture.

But the poetry of the Pléiade is true not only to the physiognomy of its age, but also to its country, that *pays du Vendomois,* the names and scenery of which so often occur in it; the great Loire, with its long spaces of white sand; the little river Loir; the healthy, upland country, with its scattered pools of water and waste roadsides, and retired manors, with their crazy old feudal defenses half fallen into decay; La Beauce, the granary of France, where the vast rolling fields of corn seem to anticipate the great western sea itself. It is full of the traits of that country. We see Du Bellay and Ronsard gardening, or hunting with their dogs, or watch the pastimes of a rainy day; and with this is connected a domesticity, a homeliness and simple goodness, by which this Northern country gains upon the South. They have the love of the aged for warmth, and understand the poetry of winter; for they are not far from the Atlantic, and the west wind which comes up from it, turning the poplars white, spares not this new Italy in France. So the fireside often appears, with the pleasures of winter, about the vast emblazoned chimneys of the time, and with a bonhomie as of little children, or old people.

It is in Du Bellay's *Olive,* a collection of sonnets in praise of a half-imaginary lady, *Sonnetz a la louange d'Olive,* that these characteristics are most abundant. Here is a perfectly crystallized specimen:

D'amour, de grace, et de haulte valeur
Les feux divins estoient ceinctz et les cieulx

S'estoient vestuz d'un manteau precieux
A raiz ardens de diverse couleur:

Tout estoit plein de beauté, de bonheur,
La mer tranquille, et le vent gracieulx,
Quand celle la nasquit en ces bas lieux
Qui a pillé du monde tout l'honneur.

Ell' prist son teint des beux lyz blanchissans,
Son chef de l'or, ses deux levres des rozes,
Et du soleil ses yeux resplandissans:

Le ciel usant de liberalité,
Mist en l'esprit ses semences encloses,
*Son nom des Dieux prist l'immortalité.**

That he is thus a characteristic specimen of the poetical taste of that age, is indeed Du Bellay's chief interest. But if his work is to have the highest sort of interest, if it is to do something more than satisfy curiosity, if it is to have an aesthetic as distinct from an historical value, it is not enough for a poet to have been the true child of his age, to have conformed to its aesthetic conditions, and

*

Olive
The Nonpareil of All Mortality

With love, with highest worth, with every grace
The heavenly fires were girt, and all the skies
Were garbed in precious raiment bright with rays
And glowing hues unknown to mortal eyes:

The world was bathed in beauty and in mirth,
The sea was calm, the wind was soft, when she
Was born who stole the glories of the earth,
The nonpareil of all mortality.

She took her color from the lily's snows,
Her locks from gold, her lips' hue from the rose;
The sun endowed her hair with radiance;

To crown their handiwork the heavens were kind
And sowed the seeds of virtue in her mind,
While gods ensured her name its permanence.

(*In A Treasury of French Poetry*. Selected and translated by Alan Conder.)

by so conforming to have charmed and stimulated that age; it is necessary that there should be perceptible in his work something individual, inventive, unique, the impress there of the writer's own temper and personality. This impress M. Sainte-Beuve thought he found in the *Antiquités de Rome,* and the *Regrets,* which he ranks as what has been called *poésie intime,* that intensely modern sort of poetry in which the writer has for his aim the portraiture of his own most intimate moods, and to take the reader into his confidence. That generation had other instances of this intimacy of sentiment: Montaigne's *Essays* are full of it, the carvings of the church of Brou are full of it. M. Sainte-Beuve has perhaps exaggerated the influence of this quality in Du Bellay's *Regrets;* but the very name of the book has a touch of Rousseau about it, and reminds one of a whole generation of self-pitying poets in modern times. It was in the atmosphere of Rome, to him so strange and mournful, that these pale flowers grew up; for that journey to Italy, which he deplored as the greatest misfortune of his life, put him in full possession of his talent, and brought out all its originality. And in effect you do find intimacy *(intimité)* here. The trouble of his life is analyzed, and the sentiment of it conveyed directly to our minds; not a great sorrow or passion, but only the sense of loss in passing days, the ennui of a dreamer who has to plunge into the world's affairs, the opposition between actual life and the ideal, a longing for rest, nostalgia, homesickness—that pre-eminently childish, but so suggestive sorrow, as significant of the final regret of all human creatures for the familiar earth and limited sky. The feeling for landscape is often described as a modern one; still more so is that for antiquity, the sentiment of ruins. Du Bellay has this sentiment. The duration of the hard, sharp outlines of things is a grief to him, and passing his wearisome days among the ruins of ancient Rome, he is consoled by the thought that all must one day end, by the sentiment of the grandeur of nothingness *(la grandeur du rien).* With a strange touch of faroff mysticism, he thinks that *le grand tout* itself, into which all other things pass and lose themselves, ought itself sometimes to perish and pass away. Nothing less can relieve his weariness. From the stately aspects of Rome his thoughts went back continually to France, to the smoking chimneys of his little village, the longer twilight of the North, *la douceur Angevine;* yet not so much to the real France, we may be sure, with its dark streets, and its roofs of rough-hewn slate, as to that other country with slenderer towers, and more winding rivers, and trees like flowers, and with softer sunshine on more gracefully proportioned fields and ways, which the fancy of the exile, and the pilgrim, and of the schoolboy far from home, and of those kept at home unwillingly, everywhere builds up before or behind them.

He came home at last, through the *Grisons,* by slow journeys; and there, in the cooler air of his own country, under its skies of milkier blue, the sweetest flower of his genius sprang up. There have been poets whose whole fame has rested on one poem, as Gray's on the *Elegy in a Country Churchyard,* or Ronsard's, as many critics have thought, on the eighteen lines of one famous ode. Du Bellay has almost been the poet of one poem; and this one poem of his is an Italian thing transplanted into that green country of Anjou; out of the Latin verses of Andrea Navagero, into French; but it is a thing in which the matter is almost nothing, and the form almost everything; and the form of the poem as it stands, written in Old French, is all Du Bellay's own. It is a song which the winnowers are supposed to sing as they winnow the corn, and they invoke the winds to lie lightly on the grain.

D'un vanneur de blé aux vents

> A vous trouppe legère
>   Qui d'aile passagère
>   Par le monde volez,
>   Et d'un sifflant murmure
>   L'ombrageuse verdure
>   Doulcement esbranlez.
>
> J'offre ces violettes,
>   Ces lis et ces fleurettes,
>   Et ces roses icy,
>   Ces vermeillettes roses
>   Sont freschement écloses,
>   Et ces oelliets aussi.

De vostre doulce haleine
Eventez ceste plaine
Eventez ce sejour;
Ce pendant que j'ahanne
A mon blé que je vanne
*A la chaleur du jour.**

That, has in the highest degree the qualities, the value, of the whole Pléiade school of poetry, of the whole phase of taste from which that school derives, a certain silvery grace of fancy, nearly all the pleasure of which is in the surprise at the happy and dexterous way in which a thing slight in itself is handled. The sweetness of it is by no means to be got at by crushing, as you crush wild herbs to get at their perfume. One seems to hear the measured falling of the fans, with a child's pleasure on coming across the incident for the first time, in one of those great barns of Du Bellay's own country, La Beauce, the granary of France. A sudden light transfigures a trivial thing, a weathervane, a windmill, a winnowing flail, the dust in the barn door; a moment—and the thing has vanished, because it was pure effect; but it leaves a relish behind it, a longing that the accident may happen again.

* Hymn to the Winds
The winds are invoked by the winnowers of corn

To you, troop so fleet,
    That with winged wandering feet,
Through the wide world pass,
And with soft murmuring
Toss the green shades of spring
    In woods and grass,
Lily and violet
I give, and blossoms wet,
    Roses and dew;
This branch of blushing roses,
Whose fresh bud uncloses,
    Wind-flowers, too.
Ah, winnow with sweet breath,
Winnow the holt and heath,
    Round this retreat;
Where all the golded morn
We fan the gold o' the corn,
    In the sun's heat.

(In *Ballads of Old France*, by *Andrew Lang*)

WINCKLEMANN

GOETHE'S fragments of art criticism contain a few pages of strange pregnancy on the character of Winckelmann. He speaks of the teacher who had made his career possible, but whom he had never seen, as of an abstract type of culture, consummate, tranquil, withdrawn already into the region of ideals, yet retaining color from the incidents of a passionate intellectual life. He classes him with certain works of art, possessing an inexhaustible gift of suggestion, to which criticism may return again and again with renewed freshness. Hegel, in his lectures on the Philosophy of Art, estimating the work of his predecessors, has also passed a remarkable judgment on Winckelmann's writings: "Winckelmann, by contemplation of the ideal works of the ancients, received a sort of inspiration, through which he opened a new sense for the study of art. He is to be regarded as one of those who, in the sphere of art, have known how to initiate a new organ for the human spirit." That it has given a new sense, that it has laid open a new organ, is the highest that can be said of any critical effort. It is interesting then to ask what kind of man it was who thus laid open a new organ? Under what conditions was that effected?

Johann Joachim Winckelmann was born at Stendal, in Brandenburg, in the year 1717. The child of a poor tradesman, he passed through many struggles in early youth, the memory of which ever remained in him as a fitful cause of dejection. In 1763, in the full emancipation of his spirit, looking over the beautiful Roman prospect, he writes: "One gets spoiled here; but God owed me this; in my youth I suffered too much." Destined to assert and interpret the charm of the Hellenic spirit, he served first a painful apprenticeship in the tarnished intellectual world of Germany in the earlier half of the eighteenth century. Passing out of that into the happy light of the antique, he had a sense of exhilaration almost physical. We find him as a child in the dusky precincts of a German school, hungrily feeding on a few colorless books. The master of this school grows blind; Winckelmann becomes his *famu-*

lus. The old man would have had him study theology. Winckelmann, free of the master's library, chooses rather to become familiar with the Greek classics. Herodotus and Homer win, with their "voweled" Greek, his warmest enthusiasm; whole nights of fever are devoted to them; disturbing dreams of an Odyssey of his own come to him. *Il se sentit attiré vers le Midi, avec ardeur,* Madame de Staël says of him, *on retrouve encore souvent dans les imaginations Allemandes quelques traces de cet amour du soleil, de cette fatigue du Nord, qui entraîna les peuples septentrionaux dans les contrées méridionales. Un beau ciel fait naître des sentiments semblables à l'amour de la patrie.*

To most of us, after all our steps toward it, the antique world, in spite of its intense outlines, its perfect self-expression, still remains faint and remote. To him, closely limited except on the side of the ideal, building for his dark poverty "a house not made with hands," it early came to seem more real than the present. In the fantastic plans of foreign travel continually passing through his mind, to Egypt, for instance, and to France, there seems always to be rather a wistful sense of something lost to be regained, than the desire of discovering anything new. Goethe has told us how, in his eagerness to handle the antique, he was interested in the insignificant vestiges of it which the neighborhood of Strasbourg contained. So we hear of Winckelmann's boyish antiquarian wanderings among the ugly Brandenburg sandhills. Such a conformity between himself and Winckelmann, Goethe would have gladly noted.

At twenty-one he enters the University of Halle, to study theology, as his friends desire; instead, he becomes the enthusiastic translator of Herodotus. The condition of Greek learning in German schools and universities had fallen, and Halle had no professors who could satisfy his sharp intellectual craving. Of his professional education he always speaks with scorn, claiming to have been his own teacher from first to last. His appointed teachers did not perceive that a new source of culture was within their hands. *Homo vagus et inconstans!,* one of them pedantically reports of the future pilgrim to Rome, unaware on which side his irony was whetted. When professional education confers nothing but irritation on a Schiller, no one ought to be surprised; for Schiller, and such as he, are primarily spiritual adventurers. But that Winckelmann, the votary of the gravest of intellectual traditions, should get nothing but an attempt at suppression from the professional guardians of learning, is what may well surprise us.

In 1743 he became master of a school at Seehausen. This was the most wearisome period of his life. Notwithstanding a success in dealing with children, which seems to testify to something simple and primeval in his nature, he found the work of teaching very depressing. Engaged in this work, he writes that he still has within him a longing desire to attain to the knowledge of beauty—*sehnlich wünschte zur Kenntniss des Schönen zu gelangen.* He had to shorten his nights, sleeping only four hours, to gain time for reading. And here Winckelmann made a step forward in culture. He multiplied his intellectual force by detaching from it all flaccid interests. He renounced mathematics and law, in which his reading had been considerable, all but the literature of the arts. Nothing was to enter into his life unpenetrated by its central enthusiasm. At this time he undergoes the charm of Voltaire. Voltaire belongs to that flimsier, more artificial, classical tradition, which Winckelmann was one day to supplant, by the clear ring, the eternal outline of the genuine antique. But it proves the authority of such a gift as Voltaire's, that it allures and wins even those born to supplant it. Voltaire's impression on Winckelmann was never effaced; and it gave him a consideration for French literature which contrasts with his contempt for the literary products of Germany. German literature transformed, siderealized, as we see it in Goethe, reckons Winckelmann among its initiators. But Germany at that time presented nothing in which he could have anticipated *Iphigenia,* and the formation of an effective classical tradition in German literature.

Under this purely literary influence, Winckelmann protests against Christian Wolff and the philosophers. Goethe, in speaking of this protest, alludes to his own obligations to Emmanuel Kant. Kant's influence over the culture of Goethe, which he tells us could not have been resisted by him without loss, consisted in a severe limitation to the concrete. But he adds, that in born antiquaries, like Winckelmann, constant handling of the antique, with its eternal outline, maintains that limitation as effectually as a critical philosophy. Plato however, saved so often for his redeeming literary manner, is excepted from Winckelmann's proscription of the philosophers. The modern most often meets Plato on that side which seems to pass beyond Plato into a world no longer pagan, based on the conception of a spiritual life. But the element of affinity which he presents to Winckelmann is that which is wholly Greek, and alien from the Christian world, represented by that group of brilliant youths in the *Lysis*, still uninfected by any spiritual sickness, finding the end of all endeavor in the aspects of the human form, the continual stir and motion of a comely human life.

This new-found interest in Plato's dialogues could not fail to increase his desire to visit the countries of the classical tradition. "It is my misfortune," he writes, "that I was not born to great place, wherein I might have had cultivation, and the opportunity of following my instinct, and forming myself." Probably the purpose of visiting Rome was already conceived, and he silently preparing for it. Count Bünau, the author of an historical work then of note, had collected at Nöthenitz, near Dresden, a valuable library, now part of the library of Dresden. In 1784 Winckelmann wrote to Bünau in halting French: He is emboldened, he says, by Bünau's indulgence for needy men of letters. He desires only to devote himself to study, having never allowed himself to be dazzled by favorable prospects in the church. He hints at his doubtful position "in a metaphysical age, when humane literature is trampled under foot. At present," he goes on, "little value is set on Greek literature, to which I have devoted myself so far as I could penetrate, when good books are so scarce and expensive." Finally, he desires a place in some corner of Bünau's library: "Perhaps, at some future time, I shall become more useful to the public, if, drawn from obscurity in whatever way, I can find means to maintain myself in the capital."

Soon afterward we find Winckelmann in the library at Nöthenitz. Thence he made many visits to the collection of antiquities at Dresden. He became acquainted with many artists, above all with Oeser, Goethe's future friend and master, who, uniting a high culture with a practical knowledge of art, was fitted to minister to Winckelmann's culture. And now there opened for him a new way of communion with the Greek life. Hitherto he had handled the words only of Greek poetry, stirred indeed and roused by them, yet divining beyond the words an unexpressed pulsation of sensuous life. Suddenly he is in contact with that life, still fervent in the relics of plastic art. Filled as our culture is with the classical spirit, we can hardly imagine how deeply the human mind was moved, when, at the Renaissance, in the midst of a frozen world, the buried fire of ancient art rose up from under the soil. Winckelmann here reproduces for us the earlier sentiment of the Renaissance. On a sudden the imagination feels itself free. How facile and direct, it seems to say, is this life of the senses and the understanding, when once we have apprehended it! That is the more liberal life we have been seeking so long, so near to us all the while. How mistaken and roundabout have been our efforts to reach it by mystic passion, and monastic revery; how they have deflowered the flesh; how little they have emancipated us! Hermione melts from her stony posture, and the lost proportions of life right themselves. Here, then, we see in vivid realization that tendency of Winckelmann to escape from abstract theory to intuition, to the exercise of sight and touch. Lessing, in the *Laokoon,* has theorized finely on the relation of poetry to sculpture; and philosophy can give us theoretical reasons why, not poetry but sculpture should be the most sincere and exact expression of the Greek ideal. By a happy, unperplexed dexterity, Winckelmann solves the question in the concrete. It is what Goethe calls his *Gewahrwerden der griechischen Kunst,* his *finding* of Greek art.

Through the tumultuous richness of Goethe's culture, the influence of Winckelmann is always discernible, as the strong, regulative undercurrent of a clear, antique motive. "One learns nothing from him," he says to Eckermann, "but one becomes something." If we ask what the secret of this influence was, Goethe himself will tell us— elasticity, wholeness, intellectual integrity. And yet these expressions, because they fit Goethe, with his universal culture, so well, seem hardly to describe the narrow, exclusive interest of Winckelmann. Doubtless Winckelmann's perfection is a narrow perfection; his feverish nursing of the one motive of his life is a contrast to Goethe's various energy. But what affected Goethe, what instructed him and ministered to his culture, was the integrity, the truth to its type, of the given force. The development of this force was the single interest of Winckelmann, unembarrassed by anything else in him. Other interests, practical or intellectual, those slighter talents and motives not supreme, which in most men are the waste part of nature, and drain away their vitality, he plucked out and cast from him. The protracted longing of his youth is not a vague, romantic longing; he knows what he longs for, what he wills. Within its severe limits his enthusiasm burns like lava. "You know"—says Lavater, speaking of Winckelmann's countenance—"that I consider ardor and indifference by no means incompatible in the same character. If ever there was a striking instance of that union, it is in the countenance before us." "A lowly childhood," says Goethe, "insufficient instruction in youth, broken, distracted studies in early manhood, the burden of schoolkeeping! He was thirty years old before he enjoyed a single favor of fortune; but as soon as he had attained to an adequate condition of freedom, he appears before us consummate and entire, complete in the ancient sense."

But his hair is turning gray, and he has not yet reached the South. The Saxon court had become Roman Catholic, and the way to favor at Dresden was through Romish ecclesiastics. Probably the thought of a profession of the Romish religion was not new to Winckelmann. At one time he had thought of begging his way to Rome, from cloister to cloister, under the pretence of a disposition to change his faith. In 1751, the papal nuncio, Archinto, was one of the visitors at Nöthenitz. He suggested Rome as a stage for Winckelmann's attainments, and held out the hope of a place in the papal library. Cardinal Passionei, charmed with Winckelmann's beautiful Greek writing, was ready to play the part of Maecenas, on condition that the necessary change should be made. Winckelmann accepted the bribe, and visited the nuncio at Dresden. Unquiet still at the word "profession," not without a struggle, he joined the Romish Church, July the 11th, 1754.

Goethe boldly pleads that Winckelmann was a pagan, that the landmarks of Christendom meant nothing to him. It is clear that he intended to deceive no one by his disguise; fears of the Inquisition are sometimes visible during

his life in Rome; he entered Rome notoriously with the
works of Voltaire in his possession; the thought of what
Bünau might be thinking of him seems to have been his
greatest difficulty. On the other hand, he may have had
a sense of a certain antique, and, as it were, pagan
grandeur in the Roman Catholic religion. Turning from
the crabbed Protestantism, which had been the weariness
of his youth, he might reflect that while Rome had reconciled itself to the Renaissance, the Protestant principle in
art had cut off Germany from the supreme tradition of
beauty. And yet to that transparent nature, with its simplicity as of the earlier world, the loss of absolute sincerity must have been a real loss. Goethe understands that
Winckelmann had made this sacrifice. Yet at the bar of
the highest criticism, perhaps, Winckelmann may be absolved. The insincerity of his religious profession was only
one incident of a culture in which the moral instinct, like
the religious or political, was merged in the artistic. But
then the artistic interest was that by desperate faithfulness
to which Winckelmann was saved from the mediocrity
which, breaking through no bounds, moves ever in a
bloodless routine, and misses its one chance in the life of
the spirit and the intellect. There have been instances of
culture developed by every high motive in turn, and yet
intense at every point; and the aim of our culture should
be to attain not only as intense but as complete a life as
possible. But often the higher life is only possible at all,
on condition of a selection of that in which one's motive
is native and strong; and this selection involves the renun-
ciation of a crown reserved for others. Which is better—
to lay open a new sense, to initiate a new organ for the
human spirit, or to cultivate many types of perfection up
to a point which leaves us still beyond the range of their
transforming power? Savonarola is one type of success;
Winckelmann is another; criticism can reject neither, because each is true to itself. Winckelmann himself explains
the motive of his life when he says, "It will be my highest
reward, if posterity acknowledges that I have written
worthily."

For a time he remained at Dresden. There his first book
appeared, *Thoughts on the Imitation of Greek Works of
Art in Painting and Sculpture*. Full of obscurities as it was,
obscurities which baffled but did not offend Goethe, when

he first turned to art criticism, its purpose was direct, an appeal from the artificial classicism of the day to the study of the antique. The book was well received, and a pension was supplied through the king's confessor. In September, 1755, he started for Rome, in the company of a young Jesuit. He was introduced to Raphael Mengs, a painter then of note, and found a home near him, in the artists' quarter, in a place where he could "overlook, far and wide, the Eternal City." At first he was perplexed with the sense of being a stranger on what was to him, spiritually, native soil. "Unhappily"—he cries in French, often selected by him as the vehicle of strong feeling—"I am one of those whom the Greeks call ὀψιμαθεῖς. I have come into the world and into Italy too late." More than thirty years afterward, Goethe also, after many aspirations and severe preparation of mind, visited Italy. In early manhood, just as he too was *finding* Greek art, the rumor of that high artist's life of Winckelmann in Italy had strongly moved him. At Rome, spending a whole year drawing from the antique, in preparation for *Iphigenia,* he finds the stimulus of Winkelmann's memory ever active. Winckelmann's Roman life was simple, primeval, Greek. His delicate constitution permitted him the use only of bread and wine. Condemned by many as a renegade, he had no desire for places of honor, but only to see his merits acknowledged, and existence assured to him. He was simple without being niggardly; he desired to be neither poor nor rich.

Winckelmann's first years in Rome present all the elements of an intellectual situation of the highest interest. The beating of the intellect against its bars, the somber aspect, the alien traditions, the still barbarous literature of Germany, are afar off; before him are adequate conditions of culture, the sacred soil itself, the first tokens of the advent of the new German literature, with its broad horizons, its boundless intellectual promise. Dante, passing from the darkness of the *Inferno,* is filled with a sharp and joyful sense of light, which makes him deal with it, in the opening of the *Purgatorio,* in a wonderfully touching and penetrative way. Hellenism, which is the principle preeminently of intellectual light—the modern culture may have more color, the medieval spirit greater heat and profundity, but Hellenism is pre-eminent for light—has always been most effectively conceived by those, who have crept into it out of an intellectual world in which the somber elements predominate. So it had been in the ages of the Renaissance. This repression, removed at last, gave force and glow to Winckelmann's native affinity to the Hellenic spirit. "There had been known before him," says Madame de Staël, "learned men who might be consulted like books; but no one had, if I may say so, made himself a pagan for the purpose of penetrating antiquity." *On exécute mal ce qu'on n'a pas conçu soi-même* *—words spoken on so high an occasion—are true in their measure of every genuine enthusiasm. Enthusiasm—that, in the broad Platonic sense of the *Phaedrus,* was the secret of his divinatory power over the Hellenic world. This enthusiasm, dependent as it is to a great degree on bodily temperament, has a power of re-enforcing the purer emotions of the intellect with an almost physical excitement. That his affinity with Hellenism was not merely intellectual, that the subtler threads of temperament were inwoven in it, is proved by his romantic, fervent friendships with young men. He has known, he says, many young men more beautiful than Guido's archangel. These friendships, bringing him in contact with the pride of human form, and staining his thoughts with its bloom, perfected his reconciliation with the spirit of Greek sculpture. A letter on taste, addressed from Rome to a young nobleman, Friedrich von Berg, is the record of such a friendship.

I shall excuse my delay, he begins, *in fulfilling my promise of an essay on the taste for beauty in works of art, in the works of Pindar. He says to Agesidamus, a youth of Locri,* ἰδέᾳ τε καλὸν, ὥρᾳ τε κεκραμένον, *whom he had kept waiting for an intended ode, that a debt paid with usury is the end of reproach. This may win your good nature on behalf of my present essay, which has turned out far more detailed and circumstantial than I had at first intended.*

It is from yourself that the subject is taken. Our intercourse has been short, too short both for you and me; but the first time I saw you, the affinity of our spirits was revealed to me. Your culture proved that my hope was not groundless; and I found in a beautiful body a soul

---

* "One is always a poor executant of conceptions not one's own"—words of Charlotte Corday before the Convention.

created for nobleness, gifted with the sense of beauty. My parting from you was, therefore, one of the most painful in my life; and that this feeling continues our common friend is witness, for your separation from me leaves me no hope of seeing you again. Let this essay be a memorial of our friendship, which, on my side, is free from every selfish motive, and ever remains subject and dedicate to yourself alone.

The following passage is characteristic:

As it is confessedly the beauty of man which is to be conceived under one general idea, so I have noticed that those who are observant of beauty only in women, and are moved little or not at all by the beauty of men, seldom have an impartial, vital, inborn instinct for beauty in art. To such persons the beauty of Greek art will ever seem wanting, because its supreme beauty is rather male than female. But the beauty of art demands a higher sensibility than the beauty of nature, because the beauty of art, like tears shed at a play, gives no pain, is without life, and must be awakened and repaired by culture. Now, as the spirit of culture is much more ardent in youth than in manhood, the instinct of which I am speaking must be exercised and directed to what is beautiful, before that age is reached, at which one would be afraid to confess that one had no taste for it.

Certainly, of that beauty of living form which regulated Winckelmann's friendships, it could not be said that it gave no pain. One notable friendship, the fortune of which we may trace through his letters, begins with an antique, chivalrous letter in French, and ends noisily in a burst of angry fire. Far from reaching the quietism, the bland indifference of art, such attachments are nevertheless more susceptible than any others of equal strength of a purely intellectual culture. Of passion, of physical excitement, they contain just so much as stimulates the eye to the finest delicacies of color and form. These friendships, often the caprices of a moment, make Winckelmann's letters, with their troubled coloring, an instructive but bizarre addition to the *History of Art,* that shrine of grave and mellow light for the mute Olympian family. The

impression which Winckelmann's literary life conveyed
to those about him, was that of excitement, intuition,
inspiration, rather than the contemplative evolution of
general principles. The quick, susceptible enthusiast, betraying his temperament, even in appearance, by his
olive complexion, his deep-seated, piercing eyes, his
rapid movements, apprehended the subtlest principles
of the Hellenic manner, not through the understanding,
but by instinct or touch. A German biographer of Winckelmann has compared him to Columbus. That is not
the happiest of comparisons; but it reminds one of a
passage in which M. Edgar Quinet describes Columbus's
famous voyage. His science was often at fault; but he
had a way of estimating at once the slightest indication
of land, in a floating weed or passing bird; he seemed
actually to come nearer to nature than other men. And
that world in which others had moved with so much
embarrassment, seems to call out in Winckelmann new
senses fitted to deal with it. He is en rapport with it;
it penetrates him, and becomes part of his temperament.
He remodels his writings with constant renewal of insight;
he catches the thread of a whole sequence of laws in
some hollowing of the hand, or dividing of the hair;
he seems to realize that fancy of the reminiscence of a
forgotten knowledge hidden for a time in the mind
itself; as if the mind of one φιλοσοφήσας ποτέ μέτ'
ἔρωτος, fallen into a new cycle, were beginning its intellectual culture over again, yet with a certain power
of anticipating its results. So comes the truth of Goethe's
judgments on his works; they are *ein Lebendiges für die
Lebendigen geschrieben, ein Leben selbst.*

In 1758, Cardinal Albani, who possessed in his Roman
villa a precious collection of antiquities, became Winckelmann's patron. Pompeii had just opened its treasures;
Winckelmann gathered its first fruits. But his plan of a
visit to Greece remained unfulfilled. From his first arrival
in Rome he had kept the *History of Ancient Art* ever
in view. All his other writings were a preparation for it.
It appeared, finally, in 1764; but even after its publication
Winckelmannn was still employed in perfecting it. It is
since his time that many of the most significant examples
of Greek art have been submitted to criticism. He had
seen little or nothing of what we ascribe to the age of

Phidias; and his conception of Greek art tends, therefore, to put the mere elegance of the imperial society of ancient Rome in place of the severe and chastened grace of the *palaestra*. For the most part he had to penetrate to Greek art through copies, imitations, and later Roman art itself; and it is not surprising that this turbid medium has left in Winckelmann's actual results much that a more privileged criticism can correct.

He had been twelve years in Rome. Admiring Germany had made many calls to him; at last, in 1768, he set out to revisit the country of his birth; and as he left Rome, a strange, inverted homesickness, a strange reluctance to leave it at all, came over him. He reached Vienna; there he was loaded with honors and presents; other cities were awaiting him. Goethe, then nineteen years old, studying art at Leipsig, was expecting his coming, with that wistful eagerness which marked his youth, when the news of Winckelmann's murder arrived. All that *fatigue du Nord* had revived with double force. He left Vienna, intending to hasten back to Rome. At Trieste a delay of a few days occurred. With characteristic openness, Winckelmann had confided his plans to a fellow-traveler, a man named Arcangeli, and had shown him the gold medals which he had received at Vienna. Arcangeli's avarice was roused. One morning he entered Winckelmann's room, under pretense of taking leave of him; Winckelmann was then writing "memoranda for the future editor of the *History of Art*," still seeking the perfection of his great work. Arcangeli begged to see the medals once more. As Winckelmann stooped down to take them from the chest, a cord was thrown round his neck. Some time after, a child whose friendship Winckelmann had made to beguile the delay, knocked at the door, and receiving no answer, gave an alarm. Winckelmann was found dangerously wounded, and died a few hours later, after receiving the sacraments of the Romish Church. It seemed as if the gods, in reward for his devotion to them, had given him a death which, for its swiftness and its opportunity, he might well have desired. "He has," says Goethe, "the advantage of figuring in the memory of posterity, as one eternally able and strong; for the image in which one leaves the world is that in which one moves among the shadows." Yet, perhaps, it is not fanciful to regret that that meeting with Goethe did not take place. Goethe, then in all the pregnancy of his wonderful youth, still unruffled by the press and storm of his earlier manhood, was awaiting Winckelmann with a curiosity of the noblest kind. As it was, Winckelmann became to him something like what Virgil was to Dante. And Winckelmann, with his fiery friendships, had reached that age, and that period of culture, at which emotions hitherto fitful, sometimes concentrate themselves in a vital unchangeable relationship. German literary history seems to have lost the chance of one of those famous friendships, the very tradition of which becomes a stimulus to culture, and exercises an imperishable influence.

In one of the frescoes of the Vatican, Raphael has commemorated the tradition of the Catholic religion. Against a strip of peaceful sky, broken in upon by the beatific vision, are ranged the great personages of Christian history, with the Sacrament in the midst. Another fresco of Raphael in the same apartment presents a very different company, Dante alone appearing in both. Surrounded by the Muses of Greek mythology, under a thicket of myrtles, sits Apollo, with the sources of Castalia at his feet. On either side are grouped those on whom the spirit of Apollo descended, the classical and Renaissance poets, to whom the waters of Castalia come down, a river making glad this other city of God. In this fresco it is the classical tradition, the orthodoxy of taste, that Raphael commemorates. Winckelmann's intellectual history authenticates the claims of this tradition in human culture. In the countries where that tradition arose, where it still lurked about its own artistic relics, and changes of language had not broken its continuity, national pride might sometimes light up anew an enthusiasm for it. Aliens might imitate that enthusiasm, and classicism become from time to time an intellectual fashion. But Winckelmann was not farther removed by language, than by local aspects and associations, from the vestiges of the classical spirit; and he lived at a time when, in Germany, classical studies were out of favor. Yet, remote in time and place, he feels after the Hellenic world, divines the veins of ancient art, in which its life still circulates, and, like Scyles in the beautiful story of Herodotus, is irresistibly attracted by it. This testimony to the authority of the Hellenic tradition, its fitness to satisfy some vital requirement of the intellect, which Winckelmann contributes as a solitary man of genius, is offered also by the general history of culture. The spiritual forces of the past, which have prompted and informed the culture of a succeeding age, live, indeed, within that culture, but with an absorbed, underground life. The Hellenic element alone has not been so absorbed, or content with this underground life; from time to time it has started to the surface; culture has been drawn back to its sources to be clarified and corrected. Hellenism is not merely an element in our intellectual life; it is a conscious tradition in it.

Again, individual genius works ever under conditions of time and place: its products are colored by the varying aspects of nature, and type of human form, and outward manners of life. There is thus an element of change in art; criticism must never for a moment forget that "the artist is the child of his time." But besides these conditions of time and place, and independent of them, there is also an element of permanence, a standard of taste, which genius confesses. This standard is maintained in a purely intellectual tradition; its acts upon the artist, not as one of the influences of his own age, but by means of the artistic products of the previous generation, which in youth have excited, and at the same time directed into a particular channel, his sense of beauty. The supreme artistic products of each generation thus form a series of elevated points, taking each from each the reflection of a strange light, the source of which is not in the atmosphere around and above them, but in a stage of society remote from ours. This standard takes its rise in Greece, at a definite historical period. A tradition for all succeeding generations, it originates in a spontaneous growth out of the influences of Greek society. What were the conditions under which this ideal, this standard of artistic orthodoxy, was generated? How was Greece enabled to force its thought upon Europe?

Greek art, when we first catch sight of it, is entangled with Greek religion. We are accustomed to think of Greek religion as the religion of art and beauty, the religion of which the Olympian Zeus and the Athena Polias are the idols, the poems of Homer the sacred books. Thus Dr. Newman speaks of "the classical polytheism which was gay and graceful, as was natural in a civilized age." Yet such a view is only a partial one; in it, the eye is fixed on the sharp, bright edge of high Hellenic culture, but loses sight of the somber world across which it strikes. Greek religion, where we can observe it most distinctly, is at once a magnificent ritualistic system, and a cycle of poetical conceptions. Religions, as they grow by natural laws out of man's life, are modified by whatever modifies his life. They brighten under a bright sky, they become liberal as the social range widens, they grow intense and shrill in the clefts of human life, where the spirit is narrow and confined, and the stars are visible at noonday; and a fine analysis of these differences is one of the gravest functions of religious criticism. Still, the broad foundation in mere human nature, of all religions, as they exist for the greatest number, is a universal pagan sentiment, a paganism which existed before the Greek religion, and has lingered far onward into the Christian world, ineradicable, like some persistent vegetable growth, because its seed is an element of the very soil out of which it springs. This pagan sentiment measures the sadness with which the human mind is filled, whenever its thoughts wander far from what is here, and now. It is beset by notions of irresistible natural powers, for the most part ranged against man, but the secret also of his fortune, making the earth golden and the grape fiery for him. He makes gods in his own image, gods smiling and flower-crowned, or bleeding by some sad fatality, to console him by their wounds, never closed from generation to generation. It is with a rush of homesickness that the thought of death presents itself. He would remain at home for ever on the earth if he could: as it loses its color and the senses fail, he clings ever closer to it; but since the moldering of bones and flesh must go on to the end, he is careful for charms and talismans, that may chance to have some friendly power in them, when the inevitable shipwreck comes. Such sentiment is a part of the eternal basis of all religions, modified indeed by changes of time and place, but indestructible, because its root is so deep in the earth of man's nature. The breath of religious initiators passes over them; a few "rise up with wings as eagles," but the broad level of religious life is not permanently changed. Religious progress, like all purely spiritual progress, is confined to a few. This sentiment fixes itself in the earliest times to certain usages of patriarchal life, the kindling of fire, the washing of the body, the slaughter of the flock, the gathering of harvest, holidays and dances. Here are the beginnings of a ritual, at first as occasional and unfixed as the sentiment which it expresses, but destined to become the permanent element of religious life. The usages of patriarchal life change; but this germ of ritual remains, developing, but always in a religious interest, losing its domestic character, and therefore becoming more and more inexplicable with each generation. This pagan worship, in spite of local variations, essentially one, is an element in all religions. It is the anodyne which the religious principle, like one administering opiates to the incurable, has added to the law which makes life somber for the vast majority of mankind.

More definite religious conceptions come from other sources, and fix themselves upon this ritual in various ways, changing it, and giving it new meanings. In Greece they were derived from mythology, itself not due to a religious source at all, but developing in the course of time into a body of religious conceptions, entirely human in form and character. To the unprogressive ritual element it brought these conceptions, itself ἡ πτεροῦ δύναμις, the power of the wing, an element of refinement, of ascension, with the promise of an endless destiny. While the ritual remains fixed, the aesthetic element, only accidentally connected with it, expands with the freedom and mobility of the things of the intellect. Always, the fixed element is the religious observance; the fluid, unfixed element is the myth, the religious conception. This religion is itself pagan, and has in any broad view of it, the pagan sadness. It does not at once, and for the majority, become the higher Hellenic religion. That primeval pagan sentiment, as it is found in its most pronounced form in Christian countries where Christianity has been least adulterated by modern ideas, as in Catholic Bavaria, is discernible also in the common world of Greek religion, against which the higher Hellenic culture is in relief. In Greece, as in Catholic Bavaria, the beautiful artistic shrines, with their chastened taste, are far between. The wilder people have wilder gods; which, however, in Athens, or Corinth, or Lacedæmon, changing ever with the worshipers in whom they live and move and have their being, borrow something of the lordliness and distinction of human nature there. The fiery, stupefying wine becomes in a happier region clear and exhilarating. In both, the country people cherish the unlovely idols of an earlier time, such as those which Pausanias found still devoutly preserved in Arcadia. Athenæus tells the story of one who, coming to a temple of Latona, had expected to see a worthy image of the mother of Apollo, and who laughed on finding only a shapeless wooden figure. In both, the fixed element is not the myth or religious conception, but the religious observance with its unknown origin, and meaning only half understood. Even the mysteries, the centers of Greek religious life at a later period, were not a doctrine but a ritual; and one can imagine the Roman Catholic church retaining its hold through the "sad mechanic exercise" of its ritual, in spite of a diffused criticism or scepticism. Again, each adjusts but imperfectly its moral and theological conceptions; each has its mendicants, its purifications, its antinomian mysticism, its garments offered to the gods, its statues worn with kissing, its exaggerated superstitions for the vulgar only, its worship of sorrow, its *addolorata,* its mournful mysteries. There is scarcely a wildness of the Roman Catholic church that has not been anticipated by Greek polytheism. What should we have thought of the vertiginous prophetess at the very center of Greek religion? The supreme Hellenic culture is a sharp edge of light across this gloom. The Dorian worship of Apollo, rational, chastened, debonair, with his unbroken daylight, always opposed to the sad Chthonian divinities, is the aspiring element, by force and spring of which Greek religion sublimes itself. Religions have sometimes, like mighty streams, been diverted to a higher service of humanity as political institutions. Out of Greek religion, under happy conditions, arises Greek art, *das Einzige, das Unerwartete,* to minister to human culture. The claim of Greek religion is that it was able to transform itself into an artistic ideal. Unlike that

Delphic Pythia, old but clothed as a maiden, this new Pythia is a maiden, though in the old religious vesture.

For the thoughts of the Greeks about themselves, and their relation to the world, were ever in the happiest readiness to be turned into objects for the senses. In this lies the main distinction between Greek art and the mystical art of the Christian Middle Ages, which is always struggling to express thoughts beyond itself. Take, for instance, a characteristic work of the Middle Ages, Angelico's *Coronation of the Virgin,* in the cloister of Saint Mark's at Florence. In some strange halo of a moon the Virgin and our Lord are sitting, clad in mystical white raiment, half shroud, half priestly linen. Our Lord, with rosy nimbus and the long pale hair (*tanquam lana alba et tanquam nix*) of the figure of the Apocalypse, sets with slender fingertips, a crown of pearl on the head of his mother, who, corpselike in her refinement, is bending to receive it, the light lying like snow upon her forehead. Certainly, it cannot be said of Angelico's fresco that it throws into a sensible form our highest thoughts about man and his relation to the world; but it did not do this adequately even for Angelico. For him, all that is outward or sensible in his work—the hair like wool, the rosy nimbus, the crown of pearl—is only the symbol or type of an inexpressible world, to which he wishes to direct the thoughts; he would have shrunk from the notion that what the eye apprehended was all. Such forms of art, then, are inadequate to the matter they clothe; they remain ever below its level. Something of this kind is true also of Oriental art. As in the Middle Ages from an exaggerated inwardness, so in the East from a vagueness, a want of definition in thought, the matter presented to art is unmanageable: forms of sense struggle vainly with it. The many-headed gods of the East, the Orientalized Diana of Ephesus, with its numerous breasts, like Angelico's fresco, are at best overcharged symbols, a means of hinting at an idea which art cannot adequately express, which still remains in the world of shadows.

But take a work of Greek art, the Venus of Melos. That is in no sense a symbol, a suggestion of anything beyond its own victorious fairness. The mind begins and ends with the finite image, yet loses no part of the spiritual motive. That motive is not lightly and loosely attached to the sensuous form, as the meaning to the allegory, but saturates and is identical with it. The Greek mind had advanced to a particular stage of self-reflection, but was careful not to pass beyond it. In Oriental thought there is a vague conception of life everywhere, but no true appreciation of itself by the mind, no knowledge of the distinction of man's nature; in thought, he still mingles himself with the fantastic, indeterminate life of the animal and vegetable world. In Greek thought the "lordship of the soul" is recognized; that lordship gives authority and divinity to human eyes and hands and feet; inanimate nature is thrown into the background. But there, Greek thought finds its happy limit; it has not yet become too inward; the mind has not begun to boast of its independence of the flesh; the spirit has not yet absorbed everything with its emotions, nor reflected its own color everywhere. It has indeed committed itself to a train of reflection which must end in a defiance of form, of all that is outward, in an exaggerated idealism. But that end is still distant; it has not yet plunged into the depths of Christian mysticism.

This ideal art, in which the thought does not outstrip or lie beyond its sensible embodiment, could not have arisen out of a phase of life that was uncomely or poor. That delicate pause in Greek reflection was joined, by some supreme good luck, to the perfect animal nature of the Greeks. Here are the two conditions of an artistic ideal. The influences which perfected the animal nature of the Greeks are part of the process by which the ideal was evolved. Those "Mothers" who, in the second part of *Faust*, mold and re-mold the typical forms which appear in human history, preside, at the beginning of Greek culture, over such a concourse of happy physical conditions as ever generates by natural laws some rare type of intellectual or spiritual life. That delicate air, "nimbly and sweetly recommending itself" to the senses, the finer aspects of nature, the finer lime and clay of the human form, and modeling of the dainty framework of the human countenance—these are the good luck of the Greek when he enters upon life. Beauty becomes a distinction, like genius, or noble place.

By no people, says Winckelmann, *has beauty been so highly esteemed as by the Greeks. The priests of a youthful Jupiter at Aegae, of the Ismenian Apollo, and the priest who at Tanagra led the procession of Mercury, bearing a lamb upon his shoulders, were always youths to whom the prize of beauty had been awarded. The citizens of Egesta, in Sicily, erected a monument to a certain Philip, who was not their fellow citizen, but of Croton, for his distinguished beauty; and the people made offerings at it. In an ancient song, ascribed to Simonides or Epicharmus, of four wishes, the first was health, the second beauty. And as beauty was so longed for and prized by the Greeks, every beautiful person sought to become known to the whole people by this distinction, and above all to approve himself to the artists, because they awarded the prize; and this was for the artists an opportunity of having supreme beauty ever before their eyes. Beauty even gave a right to fame; and we find in Greek histories the most beautiful people distinguished. Some were famous for the beauty of one single part of their form; as Demetrius Phalereus, for his beautiful eyebrows, was called* χαριτοβλέφαρος. *It seems even to have been thought that the procreation of beautiful children might be promoted by prizes; this is shown by the existence of contests for beauty, which in ancient times were established by Cypselus, King of Arcadia, by the river Alpheus; and, at the feast of Apollo of Philae, a prize was offered to the youths for the deftest kiss. This was decided by an umpire; as also at Megara, by the grave of Diocles. At Sparta, and at Lesbos, in the temple of Juno, and among the Parrhasii, there were contests for beauty among women. The general esteem for beauty went so far, that the Spartan women set up in their bedchambers a Nireus, a Narcissus, or a Hyacinth, that they might bear beautiful children.*

So, from a few stray antiquarianisms, a few faces cast up sharply from the waves, Winckelmann, as his manner is, divines the temperament of the antique world, and that in which it had delight. It has passed away with that distant age, and we may venture to dwell upon it. What sharpness and reality it has, is the sharpness and reality of suddenly arrested life. The Greek system of gymnastics originated as part of a religious ritual. The worshiper was to recommend himself to the gods by becoming fleet and serpentining, and white and red, like them. The beauty of the *palaestra,* and the beauty of the artist's studio, reacted on each other. The youth tried to rival his gods; and his increased beauty passed back into them. Ὄμνυμι πάντας θεοὺς μὴ ἑλέσθαι ἂν τὴν βασιλέως ἀρχὴν ἀντὶ τοῦ καλὸς εἶναι. That is the form in which one age of the world chose the higher life—a perfect world, if our gods could have seemed forever only fleet and serpentining, and white and red. Let us not say, would that that unperplexed youth of humanity, seeing itself and satisfied, had never passed into a mournful maturity; for already the deep joy was in store for the spirit, of finding the idea of that youth still red with life in its grave.

It followed that the Greek ideal expressed itself preeminently in sculpture. All art has a sensuous element, color, form, sound—in poetry a dexterous recalling of these, together with the profound, joyful sensuousness of motion; each of these may be a medium for the ideal; it is partly accident which in any individual case makes the born artist, poet or painter rather than sculptor. But as the mind itself has had an historical development, one form of art, by the very limitations of its material, may be more adequate than another for the expression of any one phase of its experience. Different attitudes of the imagination have a native affinity with different types of sensuous form, so that they combine easily and entirely. The arts may thus be ranged in a series, which corresponds to a series of developments in the human mind itself. Architecture, which begins in a practical need, can only express by vague hint or symbol, the spirit or mind of the artist. He closes his sadness over him, or wanders in the perplexed intricacies of things, or projects his purpose from him clean-cut and sincere, or bares himself to the sunlight. But these spiritualities, felt rather than seen, can but lurk about architectural form as volatile effects, to be gathered from it by reflection; their expression is not really sensuous at all. As human form is not the subject with which it deals, architecture is the mode in which the artistic effort centers, when the thoughts of man concerning himself are still indistinct, when he is still little pre-occupied with those harmonies, storms, victories of the unseen intellectual world, which, wrought out into the bodily form, give it an interest and significance communicable to it alone. The art of Egypt, with its supreme architectural effects, is, according to Hegel's beautiful comparison, a Memnon waiting for the day, the day of the Greek spirit, the humanistic spirit, with its power of speech. Again, painting, music, and poetry, with their endless power of complexity, are the special arts of the romantic and modern ages. Into these, with the utmost attenuation of detail, may be translated every delicacy of thought and feeling, incidental to a consciousness brooding with delight over itself. Through their gradations of shade, their exquisite intervals, they project in an external form that which is most inward in humor, passion, sentiment. Between architecture and the romantic arts of painting, music, and poetry, comes sculpture, which, unlike architecture, deals immediately with man, while it contrasts with the romantic arts, because it is not self-analytical. It has to do more exclusively than any other art with the human form, itself one entire medium of spiritual expression, trembling, blushing, melting into dew, with inward excitement. That spirituality which only lurks about architecture as a volatile effect, in sculpture takes up the whole given material, and penetrates it with an imaginative motive; and at first sight sculpture, with its solidity of form, seems more real and full than the faint abstract manner of poetry or painting. Still the fact is the reverse. Discourse and action show man as he is, more directly than the springing of the muscles and the molding of the flesh; and these poetry commands. Painting, by the flushing of color in the face and dilatation of light in the eye, and music by its subtle range of tones, can refine most delicately upon a single moment of passion, unraveling its finest threads.

But why should sculpture thus limit itself to pure form? Because, by this limitation, it becomes a perfect medium of expression for one peculiar motive of the imaginative intellect. It therefore renounces all those attributes of its material which do not help that motive. It has had, indeed, from the beginning an unfixed claim to color; but this color has always been more or less conventional, with no melting or modulation of tones,

never admitting more than a very limited realism. It
was maintained chiefly as a religious tradition. In proportion as the art of sculpture ceased to be merely
decorative, and subordinate to architecture, it threw itself
upon pure form. It renounces the power of expression
by sinking or heightening tones. In it, no member of the
human form is more significant than the rest; the eye is
wide, and without pupil; the lips and brow are not more
precious than hands, and breasts, and feet. The very
slightness of its material is part of its pride; it has no
backgrounds, no sky or atmosphere, to suggest and interpret a train of feeling; a little of suggested motion, and
much of pure light on its gleaming surfaces, with pure
form—only these. And it gains more than it loses by this
limitation to its own distinguishing motives; it unveils
man in the repose of his unchanging characteristics. Its
white light, purged from the angry bloodlike stains of
action and passion, reveals, not what is accidental in
man, but the god, as opposed to man's restless movement.
It records the first naive, unperplexed recognition of man
by himself; and it is a proof of the high artistic capacity
of the Greeks, that they apprehended and remained true
to these exquisite limitations, yet, in spite of them, gave
to their creations a vital, mobile individuality.

Heiterkeit, blitheness or repose, and *Allgemeinheit,*
generality or breadth, are, then, the supreme characteristics of the Hellenic ideal. But that generality or breadth
has nothing in common with the lax observation, the un-
learned thought, the flaccid execution, which have sometimes claimed superiority in art, on the plea of being
"broad" or "general." Hellenic breadth and generality
come of a culture minute, severe, constantly renewed,
rectifying and concentrating its impressions into certain
pregnant types. The base of all artistic genius is the power
of conceiving humanity in a new, striking, rejoicing way,
of putting a happy world of its own creation in place of
the meaner world of common days, of generating around
itself an atmosphere with a novel power of refraction,
selecting, transforming, recombining the images it trans-
mits, according to the choice of the imaginative intellect.
In exercising this power, painting and poetry have a
choice of subject almost unlimited. The range of characters or persons open to them is as various as life itself; no

character, however trivial, misshapen, or unlovely, can resist their magic. This is because those arts can accomplish their function in the choice and development of some special situation, which lifts, or glorifies a character, in itself not poetical. To realize this situation, to define, in a chill and empty atmosphere, the focus where rays, in themselves pale and impotent, unite and begin to burn, the artist has to employ the most cunning detail, to complicate and refine upon thought and passion a thousandfold. The poems of Robert Browning supply brilliant examples of this. His poetry is pre-eminently the poetry of situations. The characters themselves are always of secondary importance; often they are characters in themselves of little interest; they seem to come to him by strange accidents from the ends of the world. His gift is shown by the way in which he accepts such a character, and throws it into some situation, or apprehends it in some delicate pause of life, in which for a moment it becomes ideal. Take an instance from *Dramatis Personæ*. In the poem entitled *Le Byron de nos Jours,* we have a single moment of passion thrown into relief in this exquisite way. Those two jaded Parisians are not intrinsically interesting; they only begin to interest us, when thrown into a choice situation. But to discriminate that moment, to make it appreciable by us, that we may "find it," what a cobweb of allusions, what double and treble reflections of the mind upon itself, what an artificial light is constructed, and broken over the chosen situation; on how fine a needle's point that little world of passion is balanced! Yet, in spite of this intricacy, the poem has the clear ring of a central motive; we receive from it the impression of one imaginative tone, of a single creative act.

To produce such effects at all requires all the resources of painting, with its power of indirect expression, of subordinate but significant detail, its atmosphere, its foregrounds and backgrounds. To produce them in a pre-eminent degree requires all the resources of poetry, language in its most purged form, its remote associations and suggestions, its double and treble lights. These appliances sculpture cannot command. In it, therefore, not the special situation, but the type, the general character of the subject to be delineated, is all important. In poetry and painting, the situation predominates over the character;

in sculpture, the character over the situation. Excluded by the limitations of its material from the development of exquisite situations, it has to choose from a select number of types intrinsically interesting, interesting, that is, independently of any special situation into which they may be thrown. Sculpture finds the secret of its power in presenting these types, in their broad, central, incisive lines. This it effects not by accumulation of detail, but by abstracting from it. All that is accidental, all that distracts the simple effect of the supreme types of humanity, all traces in them of the commonness of the world, it gradually purges away.

Works of art produced under this law, and only these, are really characterized by Hellenic generality or breadth. In every direction it is a law of limitation; it keeps passion always below that degree of intensity at which it is necessarily transitory, never winding up the features to one note of anger, or desire, or surprise. In some of the feebler allegorical designs of the Middle Ages, we find isolated qualities portrayed as by so many masks; its religious art has familiarized us with faces fixed immovably into blank types of placid revery; and men and women, in the hurry of life, often wear the sharp impress of one absorbing motive, from which it is said death sets their features free. All such instances may be ranged under the *grotesque;* and the Hellenic ideal has nothing in common with the *grotesque*. It lets passion play lightly over the surface of the individual form, which loses by it nothing of its central impassivity, its depth and repose. To all but the highest culture, the reserved faces of the gods will ever have something of insipidity. Again, in the best Greek sculpture, the archaic immobility has been thawed, its forms are in motion; but it is a motion ever kept in reserve, which is very seldom committed to any definite action. Endless as are the attitudes of Greek sculpture, exquisite as is the invention of the Greeks in this direction, the actions or situations it permits are simple and few. There is no Greek Madonna; the goddesses are always childless. The actions selected are those which would be without significance, except in a divine person—binding on a sandal, or preparing for the bath. When a more complex and significant action is permitted, it is most often represented as just finished, so that eager expectancy is excluded, as in the image of Apollo, just after the slaughter of the Python, or of Venus, with the apple of Paris already in her hand. The *Laocoön,* with all that patient science, through which it has triumphed over an almost unmanageable subject, marks a period in which sculpture has begun to aim at effects legitimate, because delightful, only in painting. The hair, so rich a source of expression in painting, and, as we have lately seen, in poetry, because, relatively to the eye or to the lip, it is mere drapery, is withdrawn from attention; its texture, as well as its color, is lost, its arrangement faintly and severely indicated, with no enmeshed or broken light. The eyes are wide and directionless, not fixing anything with their gaze, nor riveting the brain to any special external object; the brows without hair. It deals almost exclusively with youth, where the molding of the bodily organs is still as if suspended between growth and completion, indicated but not emphasized; where the transition from curve to curve is so delicate and elusive, that Winckelmann compares it to a quiet sea, which, although we understand it to be in motion, we nevertheless regard as an image of repose; where, therefore, the exact degree of development is so hard to apprehend. If one had to choose a single product of Hellenic art, to save in the wreck of all the rest, one would choose from the "beautiful multitude" of the Panathenaic frieze, that line of youths on horses, with their level glances, their proud patient lips, their chastened reins, their whole bodies in exquisite service. This colorless, unclassified purity of life, with its blending and interpenetration of intellectual, spiritual, and physical elements, still folded together, pregnant with the possibilities of a whole world closed within it, is the highest expression of that indifference which is beyond all that is relative or partial. Everywhere there is the effect of an awaking, of a child's sleep just disturbed. All these effects are united in a single instance—the *adorante* of the museum of Berlin, a youth who has gained the wrestler's prize, with hands lifted and open, in praise for the victory. Fresh, unperplexed, it is the image of man as he springs first from the sleep of nature; his white light taking no color from any one-sided experience, characterless, so far as character involves subjection to the accidental influences of life. In dealing with youth, Greek art betrays a tendency even to merge distinctions of sex. The Hermaphrodite was a favorite subject from early times. It was wrought out over and over again with passionate care, from the mystic terminal Hermaphrodite of the British Museum, to the perfect blending of male and female beauty in the Hermaphrodite of the Louvre.

This sense, says Hegel, *for the consummate modeling of divine and human forms was pre-eminently at home in Greece. In its poets and orators, its historians and philosophers, Greece cannot be conceived from a central point, unless one brings, as a key to the understanding of it, an insight into the ideal forms of sculpture, and regards the images of statesmen and philosophers, as well as epic and dramatic heroes, from the artistic point of view; for those who act, as well as those who create and think, have, in those beautiful days of Greece, this plastic character. They are great and free, and have grown up on the soil of their own individuality, creating themselves out of themselves, and molding themselves to what they were, and willed to be. The Age of Pericles was rich in such characters; Pericles himself, Phidias, Plato, above all Sophocles, Thucydides also, Xenophon and Socrates, each in his own order, without the perfection of one being diminished by that of the others. They are ideal artists of themselves, cast each in one flawless mold, works of art, which stand before us as an immortal presentment of the gods. Of this modeling also are those bodily works of art, the victors in the Olympic games; yes, and even Phryne, who, as the most beautiful of women, ascended naked out of the water, in the presence of assembled Greece.*

This key to the understanding of the Greek spirit, Winckelmann possessed in his own nature, itself like a relic of classical antiquity, laid open by accident to our alien, modern atmosphere. To the criticism of that consummate Greek modeling he brought not only his culture but his temperament. We have seen how definite was the leading motive of his culture; how, like some central root fiber, it maintained the well-rounded unity of his life through a thousand distractions. Interests not his, nor meant for him, never disturbed him. In morals, as in criticism, he followed the clue of an unerring instinct.

Penetrating into the antique world by his passion, his temperament, he enunciates no formal principles, always hard and one-sided. Minute and anxious as his culture was, he never became one-sidedly self-analytical. Occupied ever with himself, perfecting himself and cultivating his genius, he was not content, as so often happens with such natures, that the atmosphere between him and other minds should be thick and clouded; he was ever jealously refining his meaning into a form, express, clear, objective. This temperament he nurtured and invigorated by friendships which kept him ever in direct contact with the spirit of youth. The beauty of the Greek statues was a sexless beauty; the statues of the gods had the least traces of sex. Here, there is a moral sexlessness, a kind of ineffectual wholeness of nature, yet with a higher beauty and insignificance of its own.

One result of this temperament is a serenity, a *Heiterkeit,* which characterizes Winckelmann's handling of the sensuous side of Greek art. This serenity is, perhaps, in great measure, a negative quality; it is the absence of any sense of want, or corruption, or shame. With the sensuous element in Greek art he deals in the pagan manner— and what is implied in that? It has been sometimes said that art is a means of escape from "the tyranny of the senses." It may be so for the spectator; he may find that the spectacle of supreme works of art takes from the life of the senses something of its turbid fever. But this is possible for the spectator only because the artist, in producing those works, has gradually sunk his intellectual and spiritual ideas in sensuous form. He may live, as Keats lived, a pure life; but his soul, like that of Plato's false astronomer, becomes more and more immersed in sense, until nothing which lacks an appeal to sense has interest for him. How could such a one ever again endure the grayness of the ideal or spiritual world? The spiritualist is satisfied in seeing the sensuous elements escape from his conceptions; his interest grows, as the dyed garment bleaches in the keener air. But the artist steeps his thought again and again into the fire of color. To the Greek this immersion in the sensuous was indifferent. Greek sensuousness, therefore, does not fever the blood; it is shameless and childlike. Christian asceticism, on the other hand, discrediting the slightest touch of sense, has from time to time provoked into strong emphasis the contrast or antagonism to itself, of the artistic life, with its inevitable sensuousness. *I did but taste a little honey with the end of the rod that was in mine hand, and lo, I must die.* It has sometimes seemed hard to pursue that life without something of conscious disavowal of a spiritual world; and this imparts to genuine artistic interests a kind of intoxication. From this intoxication Winckelmann is free; he fingers those pagan marbles with unsinged hands, with no sense of shame or loss. That is to deal with the sensuous side of art in the pagan manner.

The longer we contemplate that Hellenic ideal, in which man is at unity with himself, with his physical nature, with the outward world, the more we may be inclined to regret that he should ever have passed beyond it, to contend for a perfection that makes the blood turbid, and frets the flesh, and discredits the actual world about us. But if he was to be saved from the ennui which ever attaches itself to realization, even the realization of perfection, it was necessary that a conflict should come, that some sharper note should grieve the perfect harmony, in order that the spirit chafed by it might beat out at last a broader and profounder music. In Greek tragedy this conflict has begun; man finds himself face to face with rival claims. Greek tragedy shows how such a conflict may be treated with serenity, how the evolution of it may be a spectacle of the dignity, not of the impotence, of the human spirit. But it is not only in tragedy that the Greek spirit showed itself capable of thus winning joy out of matter in itself full of discouragements. Theocritus too, often strikes a note of romantic sadness. But what a blithe and steady poise, above these discouragements, in a clear and sunny stratum of the air!

Into this stage of Greek achievement Winckelmann did not enter. Supreme as he is where his true interest lay, his insight into the typical unity and repose of the highest sort of sculpture seems to have involved limitation in another direction. His conception of art excludes that bolder type of it which deals confidently and serenely with life, conflict, evil. Living in a world of exquisite but abstract and colorless form, he could hardly have conceived of the subtle and penetrative, but somewhat grotesque art of the modern world. What would he have thought of Gilliatt, in Victor Hugo's *Travailleurs de la Mer,* or of the bleeding mouth of Fantine in the first part of *Les Misérables,* penetrated as it is with a sense of beauty, as lively and transparent as that of a Greek? There is even a sort of preparation for the romantic temper within the limits of the Greek ideal itself, which Winckelmann failed to see. For Greek religion has not merely its mournful mysteries of Adonis, of Hyacinthus, of Demeter, but it is conscious also of the fall of earlier divine dynasties. Hyperion gives way to Apollo, Oceanus to Poseidon. Around the feet of that tranquil Olympian family still crowd the weary shadows of an earlier, more formless divine world. Even their still minds are troubled with thoughts of a limit to duration, of inevitable decay, of dispossession. Again, the supreme and colorless abstraction of those divine forms, which is the secret of their repose, is also a premonition of the fleshless, consumptive refinements of the pale, medieval artists. That high indifference to the outward, that impassivity, has already a touch of the corpse in it; we see already Angelico and the *Master of the Passion* in the artistic future. The crushing of the sensuous, the shutting of the door upon it, the flesh-outstripping interest, is already traceable. Those abstracted gods, "ready to melt out their essence fine into the winds," who can fold up their flesh as a garment, and remain themselves, seem already to feel that bleak air, in which, like Helen of Troy herself, they wander as the specters of the Middle Ages.

Gradually, as the world came into the church, an artistic interest, native in the human soul, reasserted its claims. But Christian art was still dependent on pagan examples, building the shafts of pagan temples into its churches, perpetuating the form of the basilica, in later times, working the disused amphitheaters as quarries. The sensuous expression of conceptions which unreservedly discredit the world of sense, was the delicate problem which Christian art had before it. If we think of medieval painting, as it ranges from the early German schools, still with something of the air of the charnelhouse about them, to the clear loveliness of Perugino, we shall see how that problem was solved. Even in the worship of sorrow the native blitheness of art asserted itself; the religious spirit, as

Hegel says, "smiled through its tears." So perfectly did the young Raphael infuse that *Heiterkeit,* that pagan blitheness, into religious works, that his picture of Saint Agatha at Bologna became to Goethe a step in the evolution of *Iphigenia*. But in proportion as this power of smiling was found again, there came also an aspiration toward that lost antique art, some relics of which Christian art had buried in itself, ready to work wonders when their day came.

The history of art has suffered as much as any history by trenchant and absolute divisions. Pagan and Christian art are sometimes harshly opposed, and the Renaissance is represented as a fashion which set in at a definite period. That is the superficial view; the deeper view is that which preserves the identity of European culture. The two are really continuous: and there is a sense in which it may be said that the Renaissance was an uninterrupted effort of the Middle Ages, that it was ever taking place. When the actual relics of the antique were restored to the world, in the view of the Christian ascetic it was as if an ancient plague pit had been opened: all the world took the contagion of the life of nature and of the senses. And now it was seen that the medieval spirit too had done something for the destiny of the antique. By hastening the decline of art, by withdrawing interest from it, and yet keeping unbroken the threat of its traditions, it had suffered the human mind to repose, that it might awake when day came, with eyes refreshed, to those antique forms.

The aim of a right criticism is to place Winckelmann in an intellectual perspective, of which Goethe is the foreground. For, after all, he is infinitely less than Goethe; it is chiefly because at certain points he comes in contact with Goethe, that criticism entertains consideration of him. His relation to modern culture is a peculiar one. He is not of the modern world; nor is he of the eighteenth century, although so much of his outer life is characteristic of it. But that note of revolt against the eighteenth century, which we detect in Goethe, was struck by Winckelmann. Goethe illustrates that union of the Romantic spirit, its adventure, its variety, its deep subjectivity, with Hellenism, its transparency, its rationality, its desire of beauty—that marriage of Faust and Helena, of which the art of the nineteenth century is the child, the beautiful lad Euphorion, as Goethe conceives him, on the crags, in the "splendor of battle," "in harness as for victory," his brows bound with light. Goethe illustrates, too, the preponderance in this marriage of the Hellenic element; and that element, in its true essence, was made known to him by Winckelmann.

Breadth, centrality, with blitheness and repose, are the marks of Hellenic culture. Is that culture a lost art? The local, accidental coloring of its own age has passed from it; the greatness that is dead looks greater when every link with what is slight and vulgar has been severed; we can only see it at all in the reflected, refined light which a high education creates for us. Can we bring down that ideal into the gaudy, perplexed light of modern life?

Certainly, for us of the modern world, with its conflicting claims, its entangled interests, distracted by so many sorrows, so many pre-occupations, so bewildering an experience, the problem of unity with ourselves, in blitheness and repose, is far harder than it was for the Greek within the simple terms of antique life. Yet, not less than ever, the intellect demands completeness, centrality. It is this which Winckelmann imprints on the imagination of Goethe, at the beginning of his culture, in its original and simplest form, as in a fragment of Greek art itself, stranded on that littered, indeterminate shore of Germany in the eighteenth century. In Winckelmann, this type comes to him, not as in a book or a theory, but importunately, in a passionate life or personality. For Goethe, possessing all modern interests, ready to be lost in the perplexed currents of modern thought, he defines, in clearest outline, the problem of culture—balance, unity with oneself, consummate Greek modeling.

It could no longer be solved, as in Phryne ascending naked out of the water, by perfection of bodily form, or any joyful union with the world without; the shadows had grown too long, the light too solemn for that. It could hardly be solved, as in Pericles or Phidias, by the direct exercise of any single talent; amid the manifold claims of modern culture, that could only have ended in a thin, one-sided growth. Goethe's Hellenism was of another order, the *Allgemeinheit* and *Heiterkeit*, the completeness and serenity, of a watchful, exigent intellectualism. *Im Ganzen, Guten, Wahren, resolut zu leben* is Goethe's description of his own higher life; and what is meant by life in the whole—*im Ganzen?* It means the life of one for whom, over and over again, what was once precious has become indifferent. Everyone who aims at the life of culture is met by many forms of it, arising out of the intense, laborious, one-sided development of some special talent. They are the brightest enthusiasms the world has to show. They do not care to weigh the claims which this or that alien form of culture makes upon them. But the pure instinct of self-culture cares not so much to reap all that these forms of culture can give, as to find in them its own strength. The demand of the intellect is to feel itself alive. It must see into the laws, the operation, the intellectual reward of every divided form of culture; but only that it may measure the relation between itself and them. It struggles with those forms till its secret is won from each, and then lets each fall back into its place, in the supreme, artistic view of life. With a kind of passionate coldness, such natures rejoice to be away from and past their former selves. Above all, they are jealous of that abandonment to one special gift which really limits their capabilities. It would have been easy for Goethe, with the gift of a sensuous nature to let it overgrow him. It comes naturally perhaps, with certain other worldly gifts to be even as the *Schöne Seele* in *Wilhelm Meister;* but to the large vision of Goethe, that seemed to be a phase of life that a man might feel all round, and leave behind him. Again, it is easy to indulge the commonplace metaphysical instinct. But a taste for metaphysics may be one of those things which we must renounce, if we mean to mold our lives to artistic perfection. Philosophy serves culture, not by the fancied gift of absolute or transcendental knowledge, but by suggesting questions which help one to detect the passion, and strangeness, and dramatic contrasts of life.

But Goethe's culture did not remain "behind the veil"; it ever emerged in the practical functions of art, in actual production. For him the problem came to be: Can the *Allgemeinheit* and *Heiterkeit* of the antique be communicated to artistic productions, which shall contain the fullness of the experience of the modern world? We have seen that the development of the various forms of art has corresponded to the development of the thoughts of man concerning himself, to the growing revelation of the mind to itself. Sculpture corresponds to the unperplexed, emphatic outlines of Hellenic humanism; painting to the mystic depth, and intricacy of the Middle Ages; music and poetry have their fortune in the modern world. Let us understand by poetry all literary production which attains the power of giving pleasure by its form, as distinct from its matter. Only in this varied literary form can art command that width, variety, delicacy of resources, which will enable it to deal with the conditions of modern life. What modern art has to do in the service of culture is so to rearrange the details of modern life, so to reflect it, that it may satisfy the spirit. And what does the spirit need in the face of modern life? The sense of freedom. That naive, rough sense of freedom, which supposes man's will to be limited, if at all, only by a will stronger than his, he can never have again. The attempt to represent it in art would have so little verisimilitude that it would be flat and uninteresting. The chief factor in the thoughts of the modern mind concerning itself is the intricacy, the universality of natural law, even in the moral order. For us, necessity is not, as of old, a sort of mythological personage without us, with whom we can do warfare; it is a magic web woven through and through us, like that magnetic system of which modern science speaks, penetrating us with a network, subtler than our subtlest nerves, yet bearing in it the central forces of the world. Can art represent men and women in these bewildering toils so as to give the spirit at least an equivalent for the sense of freedom? Certainly, in Goethe's romances, and even more in the romances of Victor Hugo, there are high examples of modern art dealing thus with modern life, regarding that life as the modern mind must regard it, yet reflecting upon it blitheness and repose. Natural laws we shall never modify, embarrass us as they may; but there is still something in the nobler or less noble attitude with which we watch their fatal combinations. In those romances of Goethe and Victor Hugo, in some excellent work done after them, this entanglement, this network of law, becomes the tragic situation, in which certain groups of noble men and women work out for themselves a supreme dénouement. Who, if he saw through all, would fret against the chain of circumstance which endows one at the end with those great experiences?

CONCLUSION

Λέγει που Ἡράκλειτος ὅτι πάντα χωρεῖ καὶ οὐδὲν μένει

TO regard all things and principles of things as inconstant modes or fashions has more and more become the tendency of modern thought. Let us begin with that which is without—our physical life. Fix upon it in one of its more exquisite intervals, the moment, for instance, of delicious recoil from the flood of water in summer heat. What is the whole physical life in that moment but a combination of natural elements to which science gives their names? But these elements, phosphorus and lime and delicate fibers, are present not in the human body alone: we detect them in places most remote from it. Our physical life is a perpetual motion of them—the passage of the blood, the wasting and repairing of the lenses of the eye, the modification of the tissues of the brain under every ray of light and sound—processes which science reduces to simpler and more elementary forces. Like the elements of which we are composed, the action of these forces extends beyond us: it rusts iron and ripens corn. Far out on every side of us those elements are broadcast, driven in many currents; and birth and gesture and death and the springing of violets from the grave are but a few out of ten thousand resultant combinations. That clear, perpetual outline of face and limb is but an image of ours, under which we group them—a design in a web, the actual threads of which pass out beyond it. This at least of flamelike our life has, that it is but the concurrence, renewed from moment to moment, of forces parting sooner or later on their ways.

Or if we begin with the inward world of thought and feeling, the whirlpool is still more rapid, the flame more eager and devouring. There it is no longer the gradual darkening of the eye, and fading of color from the wall—the movement of the shoreside, where the water flows down indeed, though in apparent rest—but the race of the midstream, a drift of momentary acts of sight and passion and thought. At first sight experience seems to bury us under a flood of external objects, pressing upon us with a sharp and importunate reality, calling us out of ourselves in a thousand forms of action. But when reflection begins to play upon those objects they are dissipated under its influence; the cohesive force seems suspended like a trick of magic; each object is loosed into a group of impressions—color, odor, texture—in the mind of the observer. And if we continue to dwell in thought on this world, not of objects in the solidity with which language invests them, but of impressions, unstable, flickering, inconsistent, which burn and are extinguished with our consciousness of them, it contracts still further: the whole scope of observation is dwarfed to the narrow chamber of the individual mind. Experience, already reduced to a swarm of impressions, is ringed round for each one of us by that thick wall of personality through which no real voice has ever pierced on its way to us, or from us to that which we can only conjecture to be without. Every one of those impressions is the impression of the individual in his isolation, each mind keeping as a solitary prisoner its own dream of a world. Analysis goes a step farther still, and assures us that those impressions of the individual mind to which, for each one of us, experience dwindles down, are in perpetual flight; that each of them is limited by time, and that as time is infinitely divisible, each of them is infinitely divisible also; all that is actual in it being a single moment, gone while we try to apprehend it, of which it may ever be more truly said that it has ceased to be than that it is. To such a tremulous wisp constantly reforming itself on the stream, to a single sharp impression, with a sense in it, a relic more or less fleeting of such moments gone by, what is real in our life fines itself down. It is with this movement, with the passage and dissolution of impressions, images, sensations, that analysis leaves off—that continual vanishing away, that strange, perpetual weaving and unweaving of ourselves.

Philosophiren, says Novalis, *ist dephlegmatisiren vivificiren.* The service of philosophy, of speculative culture, toward the human spirit, is to rouse, to startle it to a life of constant and eager observation. Every moment some form grows perfect in hand or face; some tone on the hills or the sea is choicer than the rest; some mood

of passion or insight or intellectual excitement is irresistibly real and attractive to us,—for that moment only. Not
the fruit of experience, but experience itself, is the end.
A counted number of pulses only is given to us of a variegated, dramatic life. How may we see in them all that is to
be seen in them by the finest senses? How shall we pass
most swiftly from point to point, and be present always
at the focus where the greatest number of vital forces
unite in their purest energy?

To burn always with this hard, gemlike flame, to maintain this ecstasy, is success in life. In a sense it might
even be said that our failure is to form habits: for, after
all, habit is relative to a stereotyped world, and mean-
time it is only the roughness of the eye that makes any
two persons, things, situations, seem alike. While all
melts under our feet, we may well grasp at any exquisite
passion, or any contribution to knowledge that seems by
a lifted horizon to set the spirit free for a moment, or
any stirring of the senses, strange dyes, strange colors,
and curious odors, or work of the artist's hands, or the
face of one's friend. Not to discriminate every moment
some passionate attitude in those about us, and in the very
brilliancy of their gifts some tragic dividing of forces on
their ways, is, on this short day of frost and sun, to sleep
before evening. With this sense of the splendor of our
experience and of its awful brevity, gathering all we are
into one desperate effort to see and touch, we shall hardly
have time to make theories about the things we see and
touch. What we have to do is to be forever curiously
testing new opinions and courting new impressions, never
acquiescing in a facile orthodoxy of Comte, or of Hegel,
or of our own. Philosophical theories or ideas, as points
of view, instruments of criticism, may help us to gather
up what might otherwise pass unregarded by us. "Philosophy is the microscope of thought." The theory or idea
or system which requires of us the sacrifice of any part of
this experience, in consideration of some interest into
which we cannot enter, or some abstract theory we have
not identified with ourselves, or of what is only conventional, has no real claim upon us.

One of the most beautiful passages in the writings of
Rousseau is that in the sixth book of the *Confessions*,
where he describes the awakening in him of the literary

sense. An undefinable taint of death had clung always about him, and now in early manhood he believed himself smitten by mortal disease. He asked himself how he might make as much as possible of the interval that remained; and he was not biased by anything in his previous life when he decided that it must be by intellectual excitement, which he found just then in the clear, fresh writings of Voltaire. Well! we are all *condamnés,* as Victor Hugo says: wc are all under sentence of death but with a sort of indefinite reprieve—*les hommes sont tous condamnés à mort avec des sursis indéfinis:* we have an interval, and then our place knows us no more. Some spend this interval in listlessness, some in high passions, the wisest, at least among "the children of this world," in art and song. For our one chance lies in expanding that interval, in getting as many pulsations as possible into the given time. Great passions may give us this quickened sense of life, ecstasy and sorrow of love, the various forms of enthusiastic activity, disinterested or otherwise, which come naturally to many of us. Only be sure it is passion—that it does yield you this fruit of quickened, multiplied consciousness. Of this wisdom, the poetic passion, the desire of beauty, the love of art for art's sake, has most, for art comes to you, proposing frankly to give nothing but the highest quality to your moments as they pass, and simply for those moments' sake.

Other MENTOR Books of Special Interest

Enjoying Modern Art *by Sarah Newmeyer.* The unconventional lives and works of great modern painters, from early French rebels to today's masters of abstraction. 81 masterpieces reproduced. (#MD211—50¢)

The Painter's Eye *by Maurice Grosser.* A brilliant analysis of techniques of painting from the Renaissance to the present, illustrated. (#M159—35¢)

The Creative Process *edited, with introduction, by Brewster Ghiselin.* Some of the greatest minds reveal how they begin and complete creative work in art, literature, etc. (#MD132—50¢)

Good Listening (revised and up-dated) *by R. D. Darrell.* Expert advice in the field of music and recording to help increase musical enjoyment. (#MD122—50¢)

Stories of Famous Operas (revised and expanded) *by Harold Vincent Milligan.* The plots, casts of characters and highlights of over 50 of the world's great operas. (#KD331—50¢)

Music and Imagination *by Aaron Copland.* The world famous composer explains the role of the imagination in composing, performing, and listening to music. (#MD261—50¢)

Books That Changed the World *by Robert B. Downs.* The fascinating histories of sixteen great books—from Machiavelli's *The Prince* to Einstein's *Theories of Relativity*—that have changed the course of history. (#MD229—50¢)